INTRODUCTION

Does a law enforcement officer indiscriminately murder someone and not face criminal charges? Does the term "Suicide by Cop" conveniently give them the right to commit a homicide and get away with it? Apparently so. I witnessed it with my own eyes.

This is the true story of my late husband Patrick, his lifelong struggle with depression, his crazy daredevil life, and the tragic events that led to his unnecessary death at the hands of law enforcement.

This book is written with a sincere effort to cast light on the recognition of mental illness, to take seriously the subtle signs of a person crying out for help, and to administer that help before it leads to tragedy.

Law enforcement always seem to work in their own corrupt network to get their way. The things that happened the day Patrick was killed were completely wrong. In writing this, I fight to defend the truth of my late husband's last moments, and the legacy of his life.

When I found out that the perpetrators did not reveal the truth to the news media, I was compelled to tell it. Since the case settled out of court for a very small amount, I did not get the chance to tell the real truth to a jury. I believe this truth is important to elucidate to give Patrick the respect he deserves. I hope that the facts I am about to reveal may benefit many, and perhaps save lives.

The names of individuals and some of the localities mentioned have been changed out of respect for the privacy of others.

C H A P T E R   1

The choices I made in my life wove their unique patterns, fabricating my destiny into a patchwork of circumstances I crafted myself, intertwined with events that tragically unraveled to a devastating loss.

Our family dysfuction was a generational hand-me-down that never wore out or went out of style. It was a timeless fashion of both physical and emotional abuse that infected the family like a genetic virus that no one could cure.

I knew my late husband Patrick since I was six years old. We both had the same grandmother, which made us quarter-cousins.

My grandmother was from Oahu. Patrick's dad Jim was conceived from a different father, who he never knew. My grandmother later married my grandfather and gave birth to my mom and aunt. My grandfather adopted, loved and raised Jim as his own. Despite my grandfather's tall domineering physique, he was a gentle and loving man, a sharp contrast to my grandmother who was a stern perfectionist and disciplinarian.

My grandmother didn't know how to be any other way. As a strong-willed woman with only a fourth grade education, she taught herself everything she knew. Her mother (my great-grandmother), was the victim of my great-grandfather's violent abuse. He was a chronic alcoholic, smoked opium, and openly cheated on his wife. Jim told us that when he lived with his grandparents, he witnessed his grandfather slamming a big rock onto his grandmother's head. He thought that his grandfather was trying to kill her. He said that he also saw him punch her all the time. He would bring other women home right in front of her. He lived in fear for his grandmother's life, since she was more a mother to him than his own. Jim's grandfather died at an early age. Though his grandmother was then relieved of her daily misery, those Jim's grandfather left behind were permanently scarred with nightmarish memories.

Witnessing her father's brutal attacks on her mother, my grandmother learned as a child that when a person was cruel they always got what they wanted. She never witnessed any display of love or gentleness in the way she was raised. It was only that you got what you wanted with intimidation, and then punishment when it wasn't perfect. And it was never perfect.

When my mom was five, my grandmother took her and my aunt to the mainland to visit her sister in San Francisco for nine months. She left Jim behind in Oahu with his grandparents. As an eight-year-old child, Jim could not understand why his mother left him and took his half-sisters instead, and he never forgot this.

Throughout his life, Jim was hurt by the obvious favoritism. Deep in his soul, the feelings of rejection and abandonment concocted themselves into a brew of intensifying anger and hatred toward his mother and sisters. Unintentionally, these feelings manifested themselves in the way he raised his own children.

Jim was very hard on his four children. He didn't know how else to be. He grew up in an environment where he was physically beaten if something he did wasn't good enough in the eyes of his mother. And nothing was ever good enough.

Patrick's parents were barely out of their teens when they married. On the surface, they looked like a model family. Patrick's mom was a gorgeous European-bred trophy wife, his dad was a NASA engineer; they lived in a beautiful house on a hillside overlooking La Jolla with a garage full of exotic cars.

None of their four children, Patrick being the oldest, were exempt from their father's incessant punishments. They constantly lived in fear. The children all felt a huge spike of anxiety when they heard the unmistakable sound of their dad's Porsche roaring into the driveway, hiding inside their bedrooms—worrying if they had done their chores adequately enough, and wondering who was going to "get it" next.

Though he was tough on his children, Jim was a kind and generous person. He was always busy and never lazy. He was good-looking, had a brilliant mind and could fix anything. He would drop whatever he was doing to help anyone he saw in need. He would stop and fix car problems for complete strangers. I always admired his tenacity and his big heart.

Patrick's mom was beautiful. She had a model figure, and was always very well dressed. She was affectionate and very loving to her children. Jim lavished her with expensive gifts. She had a softness about her that balanced the family see-saw that teetered on fear and negativity.

Patrick suffered physical and emotional abuse from a very early age, and the damage was indelible on his psyche. Both were daily rituals for Patrick and his three siblings. My dad told me he saw Jim beating Patrick when he was a small child, and thought it was too excessive. He made Jim stop. Patrick told me that when he was ten years old his dad hit him over the head with a heavy wrench after not doing something right while he was teaching him how to fix cars. Another time his dad whipped him with the end of a belt buckle just because he left a piece of hair behind in the sink after cleaning the bathroom. These are just a few of the things he told me; there were a lot more.

Patrick said that his mom witnessed almost all of the abuse. He remembered her shouting at his dad to stop, but she was sidelined by fear. Jim treated her well and she had a good life. What would happen to *her* if she took the kids and left?

Patrick didn't do especially well in school. He was a quiet kid, staring out the window most of the time, daydreaming about riding his bike in the canyon and finding frogs. School was a place he was sure he could be safe, and he relished in that peace while he was there. Teachers asking something of him was in no way the same as when his dad wanted something from him.

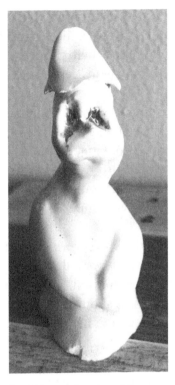

Patrick's second grade sculpture

Among Patrick's keepsakes was a clay sculpture he made in his second-grade art class. It clearly represents the silent expression of a suffering seven-year-old. It stood for his cry for love from his father that he needed and was not getting, hiding in a life of fear and inadequacy. Patrick's sculpture had alarmed his teacher so much that she initiated a parent conference. To the day he died, Patrick never had resolution to his lifelong emotional pain.

It wasn't the only time teachers wanted to speak to his parents. They often called them in regarding their concerns about injuries they saw on Patrick. His parents explained them away as a "kid just being a kid"—the injuries being due to skateboard falls, when they mostly weren't. And Patrick was ordered to rehearse and tell his teachers exactly the same thing.

6

The underpainting of denial hid itself under a masterpiece of a perfect family image thickly painted on top of it. Patrick's dad sychophantically showed off his cars, beautiful wife, and his expensive toys—for the ultimate purpose of impressing others. This facade hid his deep need to be adulated and loved. He expressed himself superficially with material possessions, and his children learned to do the same.

Jim tried to make up for the punishments to his kids. He appeased his guilt by buying them whatever they wanted, expressing his love the only way he knew how. The kids learned fast that being loved meant having material things, and the more expensive, the better. They grew up understanding that STUFF equaled love, with the pricetag as a measurement.

Patrick skateboarding in the '70s

C H A P T E R 2

Once when we were kids our families went to Disneyland together. In the days before seatbelt requirements, all the kids rolled around in the back of my dad's silver-blue Vista Cruiser. This was my earliest memory of feeling a connection to Patrick, while we were coming home from Disneyland exchanging toys and flip books. I was six and he was nine.

As we were growing up, because of family conflicts, Patrick and I rarely saw each other. Most of the time it was just on Thanksgiving or Christmas. After Patrick was old enough to drive, he wasn't around most of the time, and if he was, he was too stoned to react coherently to anyone, usually walking in late with glossed-over bloodshot eyes. He only talked if someone asked him a question. Even then I could tell he was afraid of saying the wrong thing when his dad was around. But usually his dad chose to be in the garage by himself away from everyone during family gatherings.

Though we didn't really know each other, from a distance I observed and cared about what happened to Patrick. I knew he had it tough at home. I would see him at the beach every weekend in the summer while I was in high school, but we never spoke. In high school being three years different in age seemed like a lifetime.

He was the guy everyone knew with the white Honda Civic; his car stereo boom-boxes and subwoofers facing the *outside*. His car was always parked in the front at La Jolla Shores, and it was Party Central. He and his friends would play hackysack and skateboard on the sidewalk, trying to hide their beers from the cops. My friends and I always laid out on the sand as close as we could to his music and watched him and all his friends. I felt too inadequate to even speak to him. I don't even think he knew I was there. He intimidated me.

He hung out with some crazy guys, some who later became professional skateboarders. They spent their free time breaking into people's backyards while they were on vacation and draining their swimming pools, and then blow-torching the rest of the water out so they could skate in them. They also siphoned gas from people's cars at night, did bongs all the time and stole whatever was easy.

Patrick made his living as a bartender. Sometimes my friends and I would go to the bar he worked at, just so I could watch him and see if he was okay. While he was working, high on drugs and alcohol, he looked happy. It made me feel better, even though I knew it was a cover-up. He often slept in his car to be away from his father. The bong under his front seat was his escape from reality. So was the booze that flowed freely at his bar.

Constant criticism streamed live daily whenever his dad was around, and his mother hardly intervened. The pain he felt inside turned him into a hardcore skater with a lot of anger to grind out on pool copings. When things overwhelmed him, he skated in fury, taking out his revenge on the hard concrete.

In contrast, if he wasnt skating, he was surfing. Paddling out and duck-diving under the first wave washes away whatever is bothering you, leaving it all behind on the land of stressed-out commotion. Waiting for a set and looking out to the endless horizon, you see the beginning of the wave you want and paddle for it, taking off and gliding on its magical force, wishing that feeling could go on forever. There's a peace about that that nothing compares to. You wish the waves never shut down. You wish you never got tired or hungry. But eventually the winds pick up, the tides change, or you have to go to work, and the spell is broken.

Patrick appeared to have lived his life with a subconscious death-wish. He was the king of drama on his self-made stage of passive-aggression. It was all an act to get a much needed reaction from his parents.

Patrick's consistently reckless behavior was simply a display of his need for his father's approval. He was always doing crazy things and living on the edge of disaster. All who knew him were used to it, even entertained by it, not noticing that his finger was getting closer and closer to the trigger. There were many signs hiding in the shadows of ignorance and denial that slowly materialized into a tragedy waiting to happen.

He often bragged about having "nine lives." As it turned out, he had more than that, but here are some of his potential near-misses:

1. DRIVING TO CABO
2. CONCEPTION BAY GUYS
3. ABREOJOS DEMON
4. GETTING SHOT AT
5. ALMOST ROLLING CAR
6. DRIVING MOTORCYCLE STANDING ON SEAT
7. ROLLING TRUCK
8. JUMPED WITH KNIFE
9. FREAK SURF THING

1. DRIVING TO CABO

Anyone who can make a twenty-two hour drive through Baja alone and not fear extinction is passively suicidal. If you didn't die driving off cliffs with no guardrails while the car in front of you is throwing Tecate cans out the window and a huge semi is coming right at you from the other direction on a blind corner all at the same time, then you're lucky.

Patrick told me: "I drove by myself to Abreojos and Cabo three times. Making it back each time without being buried in the desert or crashing my truck is probably because I made most of those drives totally sober, with Diet Coke, Judas Priest and Ozzy. The Mexican Federales would pull you over if they felt like it, even if you weren't breaking the "law." A lot of times I paid my way out of Mexican prison by giving the cops all the cash in my wallet. I knew to hide the rest. I kept a cooler in the back of my truck full of beers and soda. The beers weren't for me—they were for the dudes wearing heavy military uniforms who randomly stood in the road with their rifles pointed at you in the searing desert heat, in the middle of nowhere. They made you stop to search your vehicle for guns and drugs, and sometimes whatever else they wanted. The beers and soda made them a little nicer most of the time."

2. CONCEPTION BAY GUYS

"On another trip to Baja, I stopped at Conception Bay to rest. Three guys appeared out of nowhere and came up to me, asking for help with their car, but there was not another car anywhere in sight. They asked for a ride to the next gas station which was several kilometers away. I had a real bad feeling. I lied and said I had to find something to eat first and then I'd come back to help them, but I drove as fast as I could out of there. I'm sure that could have turned out a lot worse if I had been drinking."

3. ABREOJOS DEMON

"I was partying in Abreojos with some locals and I swear I saw a demon under this guy's truck. It looked like a pig covered with scales. It had small arms with wings and big curved claws. It was beckoning at me to come to it. I looked back and forth several times to make sure I wasn't hallucinating. After that I asked the guy who owned the truck to look to see if he saw it, and he saw it too! It felt like the thing was trying to get me to follow it to hell or something. That sobered me up real quick. I was supposed to stay three more days but I knew that thing was evil and I had to get outta there. I drove back home in the dark fourteen hours straight without stopping except to pour in some gas."

4. GETTING SHOT AT

"I drove to Baja for a one-day surf session. Everyone else had to work so I went by myself. I stopped alongside the road right after Rosarito and walked through a field to check out the surf. As I was standing there a bullet whizzed by my head. Then two more bullets hit the ground really close by. There was nobody around that I could see, and no houses. I thought I must be on someone's property but I wasn't going to stick around to apologize. So I ducked low and crawled real fast back to my truck, and then decided to go to K-38."

5. ALMOST ROLLING CAR

"After work one night it was raining pretty hard and I had just gotten onto the freeway from PB. I didn't see this at first, but there was this motorcycle really close in front of me with a girl sitting on the back. I was just about to hit them and I turned the wheel real fast and drove up the iceplant hill and almost hit a tree. Somehow I missed the tree but the hill was so steep I thought for sure I was gonna roll. But I didn't and I drove back down the iceplant and back onto the freeway. I was really lucky because that for sure would have been another DUI."

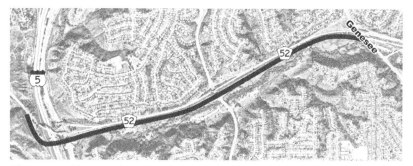

The section of freeway where Patrick and Mark stood up on their motorcycle seats.

6. DRIVING MOTORCYCLE STANDING ON SEAT

"Me and Mark were coming back from work on our motorcycles late one night and were pretty drunk. We joked about doing this before but this time we actually did it. We were coming down the hill at Ardath and then we each stood up on our motorcycle seats going around the curve that goes onto 52. We were going super fast too, all the way to Genesee."

7. ROLLING TRUCK

"I rolled two different trucks actually, once on a freeway overpass where I got another DUI. That one I don't want to talk about. This other time was on (Local Boulevard) late at night with no one around. I don't know if I passed out or what but I rolled that truck into some ditch. After that I got out and walked to my sister's house and went to sleep. When I woke up at first I didn't remember that had happened because I went outside to get into my truck and it wasn't there."

8. JUMPED WITH KNIFE

"I was walking to my car after work one night and some guy with a knife jumped me in the parking lot. I don't know—all that anger I always have inside me gave me an adrenaline rush or something because I wrestled the guy down to the ground and shoved my thumbs into his eyes until he yelled at me to stop, and then I got in my car and bailed. I guess I was lucky because he dropped the knife."

9. FREAK SURF THING

The following is an email that Patrick sent to Mark after it happened. I remember him coming home that day saying he was happy to be alive.

Date: Sunday, March 15, 1998 5:09:52 PM
From: Srfdwg
Subj: Weird scarey day
To: steffen@iglou.com

Went surfing at Scripps Sunday morning. It was 5-6' with an occasional 7-8' set coming in. Robert and I surfed that place for a while, and had some good rides. When we came in we decided to hit the La Jolla reefs, because paddling back out at Scripps was a lot of work. We checked out most of the La Jolla reefs and ended up at PB point. We were checking out the surf on the cliff when I noticed a 25-30 sailboat heading toward the reef and cliffs. I turned towards Robert and told him the Sailboat was out of control. I couldn't believe it! The sailboat went directly through a pak of long boarders almost hitting them. Lucky for them they could paddle fast enough to get out of the way. The boat hit the reef really hard and was tilted on its side, then a big wave came in and lifted the boat off the reef and someone came up from down below inside the boat, and turned the boat back out to sea. I couldn't believe the guy pulled it off. The boat lost the dingy it was towing and it washed up on the rocks. After that experience we went back to Wind "n" Sea and paddled out at Simmon's reef. It was about 6-7' and the tide was high. Robert made it past the inside which was breaking very hard on the reef. I wasn't so lucky, and I got crunched by two waves. The next thing I knew I was getting really close to a huge rock shelf that was sticking out of the water about a foot. It was to my left and I was being sucked closer to the shelf and cliffs behind me. There was absolutely no beach only rock bluffs, and when the waves hit the bluffs it was slamming damn hard. As it turned out my situation only got worse and I was getting closer to were the waves were slamming against the rocks. By this time I was so tired I couldn't really go anywhere, only just try to stay away from where the waves were smashing against the huge rock bluffs. I tried to look for a place to come in but their was none. A few times I was pushed only 5' from the huge rocks. During this time a large crowd of people were watching me from the top of the cliffs. Dude I was fricking scared to death! At one point I thought it was completely hopeless for me, and it felt like I had no energy left in me to fight for my life. I realized this was a real life or death situation here. I kept getting battered by the waves and then their was a short lull. As I was getting swept further down, a deep cut between the huge rock bluffs appeared. It was 6' wide a 12' high and about 30' long.

Someone from the cliff yelled, "pull your leash off and swim over there". I hung onto my board and paddled as hard as I could between the bluffs before more waves came in. I kept paddling and at the end I saw a small patch of cobble stones were I could seek protection. I fricking made it! But I couldn't get out of were I was. By this time the Lifeguards showed up. A Wind "n" Sea local went to get a rope to pull me out. The walls were

vertical and I couldn't climb out. The only way out was up. Some guys threw the rope down and pulled me out. I felt embarrassed and relieved. Robert had some trouble getting in, but he paddled farther North to avoid the rocks. When I got in I was shaking. I had to thank God he was watching me. I only got a few scratches.
You know what was really weird my board never got a ding.

Patrick and Mark

Below:
Baja trips

CHAPTER 3

In my life right before Patrick, I was married to my high school sweetheart. He graduated Aviation Officer Candidate School in Pensacola, and earned his wings the year we were married.

It was the first time I had ever left (So Cal). He flew during Operation Desert Storm and was away for six months or more at a time. I was alone in strange towns where I didn't know anyone. It was during this time I got to know myself a lot better. I was an avid runner, and had ran several marathons and 10Ks that allowed me many hours of introspection about who I was, and what I wanted out of life.

I always knew that my husband was controlling and didn't express emotions or talk much, but I was holding dearly onto this fairy-tale belief that by being married to him I would somehow change him into what I wanted and needed him to be—someone who would communicate his emotions, and someone who would explore the world with me. He didn't even want to go on a honeymoon, so we didn't. I couldn't forget that.

After he served his duty as a Naval Aviation Officer, he got out and we moved back to (So Cal). Shortly after, he was hired as a Deputy Sheriff for the County of (So Cal).

It was during the first year of his induction as a sheriff and into the eighth year of our marriage that I had the ephiphany that would change the course of my life.

CHAPTER 4

A layer of sage scented mist dissolved into the first light of morning as I ran out of the cold darkness of the canyon floor and up the steep ridge to the orange glow of the sun rising over the mountains. It was a run the same as every other day before work, except this particular morning was one I would never forget. My mind and body were in a heightened endorphine state, and I saw a vision of my future.

The sweat tingled on my face and a chill energized my body into a sprint. Deep down the disappointment I had been suppressing for so long erupted with a force that I could no longer ignore. A voice very clear within me then said—*"There is so much more to life than this."* This voice knew that I had been trying to keep something together against everything that was driving it apart. It spoke of two people who wanted different things out of life.

There was a finality in my mind to the truth that I had been running away from for the past eight years. I finally realized that it was impossible to change the way a person *is.*

Two years before, I thought that having a baby would fix our marriage. It kind of did, temporarily. But after the baby stage wore off, everything returned to the same controlling dictatorship. Right after that, I thought that buying a brand new house would fix it. But that didn't work either. I only lived in that house for six months before I left.

What did I need? I was thirty years old with a two-year-old daughter and I was still trying to figure that out. What I did know was that I wanted to go places. I wanted someone who was as excited about that as I was, not someone who wished to stay on the couch forever with the remote control glued to his hand. I wanted to feel that I was an equal part of the marriage, not a servant having to fulfill another's wishes while abandoning my own. I learned quickly that expectations are a harbinger of disappointment when they are reliant on the actions of someone else.

———————————

At the same time, Patrick's life was in upheaval as well. His girlfriend he was planning to marry had just broken up with him again, this time for good.

It was Patrick's one-year anniversary with his girlfriend, and to celebrate he made dinner reservations at a very expensive restaurant. When the time came for him to pick her up, he didn't show. For more than an hour she couldn't get ahold of him. When he finally got the phone, he was so drunk and stoned that he had entirely forgotten about their dinner reservations. She was very upset, and they ended up not going at all. Her father did not want her to be with him anyway. He said to her, *"What kind of future does this guy have? He's a bartender!"* and that reinforced her decision to break it off for good.

Patrick was so distraught from the breakup that he went deeper into a self-destructive substance abuse binge that resulted in him being fired from his bartending job.

After that he was without an income, and was forced to live with his parents. His dad had agreed to this—but only under the condition that he stayed completely sober. Jim told him that if he stayed sober, he would pay all of Patrick's college and living expenses—if he finished his bachelor's degree and graduated.

It wasn't comfortable going back to the house that harbored so many painful memories. It was as Patrick described "like hell" living there again. He was still verbally abused and criticized for almost everything he did. His mom, as usual, looked the other way. Now that Patrick was an adult, his dad learned that physically he could no longer raise a hand to his son. The first time he tried, Patrick pushed him back into the wall and thought to punch him, but his dad backed down, intimidated by the anger that raged in his son's eyes.

But true to form, Jim still had to get his way and be in control, so he instead made Patrick a slave, giving him difficult chores like digging up a twenty-five foot giant Bird of Paradise tree next to their driveway all by himself. This was hard to do and very time consuming, having to do this along with all of his academic studies. After he was done with that job, Jim immediately gave him another. It was passive punishment. Patrick hated yard work for the rest of his life after that.

Almost against his will, Patrick remained quiet, and disciplined himself to focus on his college degree so he could get out of there as soon as possible—to graduate and leave his dad's control once and for all.

CHAPTER 5

In the years that followed, I would see Patrick sometimes at Thanksgiving or Christmas, and he was usually pretty stoned, or just didn't show up, so we never talked much.

One night I went to visit my mom and dad. I walked in and was very surprised to see Patrick. He had randomly stopped by to say hello to my parents just a few minutes before. As I was walking in I heard him proudly telling them that he was living totally sober, and was just about ready to graduate with a degree in Environmental Science.

That night I remember sitting on the floor looking up at him while we talked in my parents' living room. He looked good. His eyes were bright and clear, not glassy and bloodshot like I always saw them before. He was excited about graduating and was working an internship at an environmental lab. We talked about Disneyland, '80s bands, and people we both knew. I told him I had a two-and-a-half-year-old daughter and that I was getting a divorce. That was the first time I had ever really talked to him.

He was into running too, so we made plans to run together. After that we started hanging out all the time. After he graduated, we started living together. I was constantly watching him to see if he was still reckless underneath the guise of getting-to-know-you good behavior. He wasn't getting stoned anymore. He was sincere, and very kind to me. He also was excited about traveling. Over the course of six months we knew that we were falling in love. We also knew that our families would not like that. Both sides tried to talk us out of it and we defiantly ignored them.

A year later, Patrick got his dream job as a Health Inspector working for the County of (So Cal) Environmental Health

Department. We got married the same year. On our honeymoon in Cancun, we were mesmerized by the calm, warm turquoise water and white sand. We never wanted to leave. That marked the beginning of our obsession with traveling.

We would travel three to four times a year, trying to combine surfing and scuba diving on the same itinerary, but doing that usually didn't give us the best of each. We didn't want "fish tank" diving, we sought to dive open ocean with sharks: bulls, tigers, hammerheads, and great whites. We also wanted our own waves, not those everyone else was trying to catch. The best waves were on remote surf camp trips and the best diving was on dive liveaboards, and both came with much bigger pricetags. We were obsessed, and we had the money (at the time). We would come home from a trip, and right away book our next trip to have something new to look forward to. We were addicted, and excitedly kept the high going.

We were both working hard in our careers. I was in the prime of my career as a graphic designer. I owned my own business, and was blessed with prosperity. Patrick loved his job and his co-workers. We both did very well financially.

Things were too good to be true. Those years were effortless, and it was the marriage of my dreams. He worshipped me. I worshipped him. For thirteen years we lived a great life. I would be out running and be thinking that I couldn't believe that all of it was real. We were so happy. We were going wherever we wanted. We bought whatever we wanted. A lot of stuff were things that we totally didn't need. At one time, we had thirty-two surfboards. No two people need *that many* boards. We had more than fifty sets of fins, buying them because they had cool designs. Then we would find boards that complemented them, and put them together like art forms. There are some boards in our collection that we never surfed on, we just put them together to look at and admire.

We woke up early every Friday, Saturday and Sunday morning to go surfing, even when it was raining. That was our ritual. We did everything together whenever we weren't working.

Sometimes we would stay at home and play-act Pulp Fiction scenes. That movie came out the year we were married, and we both loved it. We memorized all the dialogues in the entire movie. When Patrick was buzzed, he was so happy, and always told me how much he loved me. I never got tired of hearing that. I loved it when he was like that, but at the same time always wished he would not cross that wavering line to drunkenness.

GOOD TIMES

Pat filming Bull and Lemon Sharks- Bahamas

Nicaragua

Cane Toads- Micronesia

Great White (we're inside a cage)
Guadalupe Island

Barracuda- Honduras

Lighthouse Reef, Belize   *Our Local Skatepark*

Zippers, Cabo

Galapagos Aggressor

CHAPTER 6

Underneath an intimidating barrier of self-protection, Patrick was a gentle and very sensitive person. Many did not know that about him, because their first impression of him was usually their interpretation of his abrupt sarcasm. He would talk with a straight face, making most people believe he was being serious. Sometimes he was. It was his frontline of defense with people he didn't know. It was like he approached everyone *expecting* them to criticize him. Some people are able to figure this out, and when they "get him", Patrick's guard goes down. Those who understand Patrick love him. But way too often he is misunderstood.

Patrick was totally cool to everyone, especially complete strangers. He spoke the universal language of kindness. He befriended all the locals in the foreign lands we went, with respect and profound generosity that bridged all language barriers. He always approached the local people in the lands visited as if he had known them his entire life. The spontaneous, genuine sincerity he expressed was a wide-open window to his heart. Some of the more guarded of those we encountered later turned out to be the hosts of many of our greatest adventures. We got to experience the best of their homelands, above and below the waves. He had a way with people—they easily understood his loving spirit by the gestures of his kindness.

Patrick was the only person I ever knew who made friends with people after first saying, *"Fuck you."* You had to be looking at him when he said it. His eyes laughed at you. You wouldn't expect it, but a lot of people immediately liked him. When he was happy, he made everyone around him happy.

The word *fuck* was a part of almost everything Patrick said. In some of the most remote places we went, if the locals didn't understand English, they always understood Patrick when he said *fuck*. That word is so utilitarian. It is perhaps the most versatile word in all human language. You could put any noun, verb or phrase behind or before it to perfectly define something without further explanation.

A lot of times before anyone could see that Patrick was openly generous, he was openly insane. We were driving through Waianae in Oahu once in our rented Jeep with my friend and her husband who lived on the other side of the island. Waianae isn't supposed to be a tourist destination, which meant all the Waianae locals knew when someone or something didn't belong, and trespassers were definitely not greeted with alohas. But when almost the entire community of Waianae saw what Patrick was attempting to do, all eyes were on us.

When the rules say not to do something, Patrick usually has to see why. With our rented Jeep, Patrick sped past the end of the paved road, past the sign that read END OF ROAD - DO NOT ENTER, and onto a narrow dirt path that teetered on the side of a steep cliff. It was so narrow that one side of the Jeep had to drive tilting at an angle on the side of the mountain. My friend and her husband were yelling at him not to do it. He ignored them, and was doing it anyway. He could have rolled us all over the cliff so easily if he had hesitated. We were all screaming at him, panicked, but thrilled at the same time. We came to a very small flat area where Patrick stopped and shoved the Jeep into reverse, since there wasn't enough room to turn around. I saw rocks toppling over the cliff inches beside us. He drove in reverse the entire way out, which was much scarier than driving in! We backed into the crowd that had gathered at the end of the paved road. They were yelling and cheering. My friend, her husband and I were in shock, thankful for being alive. Patrick seemed strangely composed. It was like he had a foreknowledge that everything would be fine.

Right after, we stopped at the liquor store close by and Patrick bought two cases of beer for the locals. Then we drove back to my friend's house and we were all kind of hungry so we went to get ahi poke.

At first, Patrick's spontaneous generosity kind of annoyed me. I was not so ready to give our brand new $85 language interpreter to a random taxi driver in Panama, but Patrick grabbed it out of my hand and said, "He needs it more than we do." He was right. The taxi driver guy was so stoked, and seeing his reaction made it so worth it. Over time, Patrick's generosity blessed us with enduring friendships in lands half a world away. We found great joy in going back to bring people things they wanted or needed that were hard to find in their localities. The smiles on their faces and their gratitude each time we returned gave us such a high off of giving.

Patrick's generosity was the same when we were home. One time he bought the booze for a guy in line in front of him at 7-11 that had just discovered he had forgotten his wallet.

Patrick loved building custom skateboards for the neighborhood kids. It didn't matter if we didn't know their parents. He only cared about the reaction of those kids when he surprised them with a totally brand-new skateboard. He even tuned each board according to the type of skating each kid liked to do. When we watched any of them finally doing a perfect Ollie, it made us smile at each other.

Patrick would go blowtorch water puddles out of the pools at the skateparks after it rained. He also brought tripod lights so that whoever wanted to could skate at night. The skaters loved him.

Patrick was also known as "Toad". He loved frogs and toads, and somehow word got around, and an article about him appeared in our (SoCal) County newspaper. We had frogs living in our pond in the backyard, and frogs and toads as pets inside our house. We had pet turtles and geckos as well. Patrick could identify what species of frog or toad one was by the sound of their calling. He took hundreds of excellent photos of amphibians, insects, and other small creatures. In his spare time, he evaluated frogs and toads as a volunteer for Frog Watch, a national non-profit. He took me along, wading through ponds and mud together several times a week during active seasons.

Because of his genius father, Patrick knew how to fix everything. His memories of the consequences of inadequacy prompted perfection in everything he did. If he didn't at first know how to fix something, he quickly figured out how, and then crafted that challenge with precision. Like his dad, he would stop whatever he was doing to fix anything for anyone that he saw in need. He loved fixing stuff. The only thing he was unable to fix was himself.

I hated it when he got too drunk and became reckless and irresponsible. Once he was on that course, I could never stop him. There were times Patrick got so drunk, he was the spotlight of very odd behavior in public. His actions were not understood by almost everyone, and that forced me to be with him on the stage of his crazy drama. There were countless times I had to escort him off and close the curtain. It was so embarrassing that I just wanted us to disappear. The more drunk he became, the more unpredictable and ignorant he was to anyone's intervention.

A couple of times I pretended that I didn't know him, especially when he dressed up like it was Halloween and went to the bar. It was springtime, nowhere near Halloween. When I would tell him about what he did after he sobered up, he'd say "Fuck them, I don't care."

currents

arts • life • style • tv

EYES C
To win an l
come up v
makes peop
the

Frog heaven

Frog watcher and collector **Patrick Sharp** with Froggy, a White's tree frog. *K.C. Alfred / Union-Tribune*

Local members of Frogwatch USA keep tabs on amphibian population

By John Wilkens, STAFF WRITER

As darkness arrives, **Patrick Sharp** steps over a wooden rail near Moonlight State Beach in Encinitas and then into a rock-strewn drainage ditch known as Cottonwood Creek. He has a notebook in one hand, a flashlight in the other and a thermometer in his pocket.

"Just another crazy person looking for frogs," he says.

He takes out the thermometer and measures the air temperature. He writes it on a sheet provided by Frogwatch USA, a group that monitors amphibian populations across the country.

Sharp glances at the trees to see how windy it is. He records that. It hasn't been raining recently, so he

SEE **Frogs D2**

Patrick Sharp recorded the temperature and other conditions in a drainage ditch near Moonlight State Beach as he prepared to monitor the frog population. *Earnie Grafton / Union-Tribune*

Here are a few examples of Patrick's unusual behavior:

1. HOT GUY
2. WEARING W16 TO BAR
3. LOST IN BARRIO
4. BEACH PARTY BAIL OUT
5. THERE BUT NOT THERE
6. CRASHING CHRISTMAS PARTY

1. HOT GUY

We were on vacation in Cabo. Patrick was super drunk and walked up to some guy and told him he was HOT, and he wasn't referring to the weather. The dude did not take it as a compliment, and said, "What are you, gay?" and then shoved Patrick. I said to the hot guy, "he's really drunk so don't mind him, and anyway, he's right." Then the guy left him alone. After that I had to make sure we avoided him the rest of the time we were there.

2. WEARING W/G TO BAR

I have this super blonde wig that I had once used for a Halloween costume. Patrick took it, put it on and said, "Let's go to (Local Beach Bar)". It was nowhere near Halloween. It was funny at first, but once we got there he started acting crazy. He pranced around the bar flailing his arms around, holding his beer and talking really loud, saying stuff like, "Look at that hot girl over there. Hey, HEY YOU! You're HOT! Your friend is Hot too! Hey, I'll buy everyone a round!" Everyone was watching him, and I was wishing I didn't know him. I had to get him out of there fast. He was making a big scene, but at least he was really nice to everyone.

3. LOST IN BARRIO

We were supposed to drive up and join my family on a weekend trip to Yosemite. To get there when everyone else did, I knew we needed to leave around 2 pm. Patrick was in the garage all day racing people on his Playstation. After that he fell asleep inside our van in the garage. When the time was near that we had to go, I went in to wake him and get him going. He was really drunk and stoned. He said, "Later, later." I said, "No. I don't want to have to drive in the dark, so we should leave within an hour." He got up and went to get another beer, and I thought he was going to listen to me, but instead he went back in the van and passed out again. I was trying to remain patient, but he was not hearing anything I was saying, and not caring or noticing how agitated I was becoming. He was super drunk, rude and careless, completely ignoring my feelings. It was like dealing with an obstinate two-year old. We finally left our house at 11:15 pm. Of course I had to drive now because he was way beyond wasted. At that time sections of Freeway 5 and 405 were closed for construction late at night and there were some detours. Trying to navigate through one of the detours I became full-on lost in the middle of East LA. I needed Patrick's help with the GPS that was driving us in circles, and I was frustrated and getting very upset.

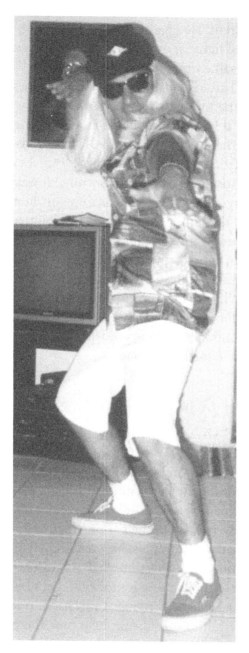

Patrick's bar attire

He was incoherent. He giggled and said, "Fuck it, I don't give a fuck... ah, you'll figure it out." This made me even more pissed off, and at the same time, scared and desperate. He was in such a stupor that I had to stop and get out to ask a local, and at that time of night the locals that were on the street weren't exactly church people. If I had been robbed, raped or gone a long time I don't think Patrick would have noticed. With God's help, I found my way out of the detour without further incident. We ended up arriving at Yosemite at 5 in the morning. It was a good thing I had called my mom and dad before we left home to prepare them for what the family was going to encounter. Patrick was a total mess, and again an embarrassment that was beyond an excuse. He didn't attend any of the family recreations while we were there. He stayed inside the van in the driveway, drinking and sleeping. Why did he even go? Because I didn't want to drive that distance alone (even though I actually *did*). Nor did I want to leave him alone at home when he was that messed up. I always feared he was potentially suicidal.

4. BEACH PARTY BAIL OUT

We had planned a beach party for my mom's birthday, and there were going to be guests there that we would be meeting for the first time. In preparation for this, Patrick and I loaded the van with all the stuff for the party, and left for the beach. When we got there he helped me set up everything, but after he was done helping me he went back to the parking lot and went to sleep in the van. A few years before this, he would have gone out surfing and hung around with me. But that was then. I kept going back and forth to the parking lot to try to get him to come out. When the guests started arriving, I ran back to the van again, and pleaded with him to PLEASE help me! There were twenty people coming, and he was supposed to be in charge of the grill. He just mumbled and said that he wasn't going to come out. He stayed in the van the entire day, ignoring me, my family and our

34

guests. I was embarrassed and upset, left with all the food to grill, and I was super stressed out because I wasn't a grill person. For me that was always a guy thing. One of my girlfriends without a word came to my rescue. Between the two of us we pulled it off, without needing to provide a dramatic excuse for the absence of my husband. It was easier for me to lie and say he wasn't feeling well. It was a situation that would have been so much worse if it weren't for my friend's intuition and that she was familiar with his erratic behavior.

5. THERE BUT NOT THERE

One of my ad agency office parties was held at a restaurant. Patrick did not want to go, but I needed him come with me because it was a dinner party where everyone was bringing their significant other. Everyone knew I was married, so if he didn't go with me I would have to come up with a lie as to why my husband was not there. But I convinced him to come along so that I wouldn't have to lie. At first, Patrick acted normal, and even talked to some of my co-workers sitting near us. Our food came, and as we started to eat, Patrick got up and left the table. I thought he was going to the restroom, but after several minutes went by and he didn't return, people started noticing, and so I asked one of the guys to go check the men's room. He came back saying no one was in there. I got up and looked outside. I saw Patrick waiting to cross the street in the opposite direction from the restaurant. I came back to the table and had to think of what to say. Everyone was asking about him, and I said I saw him outside. They asked if he was okay, and I told them that he just bails sometimes. He didn't smoke so I couldn't use that for an excuse, although I could have lied right then. I knew they were all thinking it was weird. I could not hide his strange and rude behavior and I was so uncomfortable. I wished we would have never gone. His behavior always left people gossiping and I hated it.

6. CRASHING CHRISTMAS PARTY

We were both invited to my friend's White Elephant Christmas party, and at the last minute Patrick told me he did not want to go. I went on without him, and during that time Patrick got really drunk at home. Then he decided he was going to go to the party after all. Two hours after the party started, he charges through my friend's front door, shouting, "Hey what about me!" right in the middle of the gift exchange. It was quite embarrassing for me, because he was super loud and acted really obnoxious. He was really wasted, and didn't give a crap what anybody thought of him. Luckily most of my friends were used to his strange behavior. A lot of the other guests weren't though, and when they asked me, "What's up with him?" I said, "Oh he just does weird things when he's drunk." Needless to say, we didn't stick around long after that, even though I wanted to stay and talk to all my friends. Instead I drove both of us home so I would avoid further embarrassment.

CHAPTER 7

Things had to be wrong in order for life to feel right. If something that happened was too good to be true, Patrick messed it up with negative thoughts that conformed to the reality he'd always known. It was the comfortable norm.

I decided that it was more of a struggle for me to repel his vices, so I adopted them instead. I drank along with him. In the true need to be close to him, and cope with him, I shared in his habit. If I didn't, I thought I would be completely alienated from his life. All I wanted was for us to be how we were before.

Patrick was in and out of drug and alcohol treatment programs since he was old enough to drive. It was a reccuring pattern every two to four years. He would stay sober for awhile, but eventually something would set him off, and he would say, "Fuck this!" Most of the time that trigger was the negative way his dad or someone else had treated him.

I attended a lot of the meetings with him. I saw the same patterns over and over again—people trying to give up something, and replacing it by indulging in something else. There were chain smokers and donut hoarders and caffeine bingers outside the doors, the very same people walking back inside talking about trying to give up things that were wrecking their lives. The dialogues were always the same. People hurting inside, finding false comfort in something outside that would ease the pain, but by indulgence only made it worse.

In some of the meetings the spouses or significant others were encouraged to speak. The groups addressed our co-dependant behavior, with regard to our experiences with the addict. I remember telling them more than once, "When he's drunk it's the only time he tells me how much he loves me. I hate to say this, but I selfishly rather that he be drunk and happy than sober and miserable. If he was abusive and hurting me, that is different. But Patrick never raised a hand to me. He is happy and loving and spontaneous, and so fun when he is buzzed. Just not drunk. That's when I get worried. Then it's like taking care of a two-year-old from hell."

I thought the meetings made people feed off each other by comparison: "Oh, I'm not as fucked up as you"—which made it okay for you to not be as fucked up as them. The meetings work—when you want them to. It just didn't work long enough for him. Change comes about when we *want* to do something, not when we're forced to. Perhaps we were both in denial. I just wanted him to be happy and to love me. And he just wanted to be loved by his father. If he had to be fucked up to tell me that he loved me, then I selfishly wanted that. If he had to be fucked up to forget about how he wished his father loved him, then I wanted that for him.

I did my best to postpone his inevitable self-destruction. I tried to distract him from it by going on adrenaline vacations—surfing at magazine and surf movie destinations, and diving like the kind you see on National Geographic. You can't be wasted or you would die doing the stuff we did. You can't be drunk or hung over when you're ninety feet deep hanging out with bull sharks as big as school buses. Or when you're sixty feet deep in Tuamotu in an eight knot current that would rip the mask right off your face. Or surfing where the razor-sharp reef was sometimes only a few inches beneath your board. We got stuck in quicksand once. After the initial panic, we were able to struggle out by the mercy of our surfboards. We had so many unique and rare experiences. We were really happy during those times.

We had the money, well, at first. We both did very well in our careers, but starting in 2009, two of my major clients began to trim their expenses, and within a year I ended up losing them. I didn't want to make a big deal about it because I didn't want to give up our lifestyle. We had become addicted to vacations, and ignorant to the consequences of not being able to pay for them. Soon, this began taking its toll on our bank accounts. That compelled me to work even harder. Fortunately, I still had a lot of work.

I was so focused on working to get out of debt, that I built up a wall of ignorance around everything outside of it. This included my family, and unintentionally, Patrick. On some occasions I wouldn't go to family gatherings because I had so much work to do. That was always okay for Patrick, because he didn't ever want to go anyway. If he did, he stayed away, just like his dad did when we were kids. Patrick would stay in our van parked outside my sister's house, while my family and I were inside having a good time. Since the rest of my family was familiar with his dad's behavior, this came as no surprise.

Patrick started saying that all I did was work. I told him, "Well I have to, unless you don't want to go anywhere." He always agreed, and found something else to occupy his time, and that wasn't hard—there was always a car or something around the house to fix. I was blind to everything except trying to pay our bills, keeping quiet about the problem our travel addiction was becoming.

Through the fog of my denial I began to see a warning light blinking far away in the misty darkness, becoming larger and more clear as time progressed toward it. I tried to look away, but sometimes I would wake with anxiety and worry in the middle of the night. Nonetheless, I kept my mouth shut and our bags packed. I didn't want to tell Patrick we should cut back. I wanted to stay on the level we were used to. We had to keep the high going. We continued to book trips, and found ways of offsetting paying for them with credit card balance transfers. I didn't want Patrick to worry. I knew the vacations really helped distract him from his depression, so I financed his happiness.

Because I was always working, it became a habit to live apart in the same house. On the weekends while I worked, he skated or raced. He built a totally realistic Playstation racecar system in our garage with real racecar parts—a push-button shift steering wheel, gas and brake pedals, and a custom seat, including the harness seatbelt. It was so cool and he was really proud of it. Actually, I was too. As you were driving it, the steering wheel shook as if you were on the actual terrain. He had a 3D TV and surround-sound system, racing with people all around the world, through all hours of the night.

We had a neighbor named Anna that always meditated on the grass by our house. She was just a little older than my daughter. She was into crystals, aliens, and spiritual stuff. She was always happy. Patrick started hanging out with her. She seemed to mellow him out. I thought it was good, maybe she would distract him from negative thinking.

Friday was his usual day off because he worked twelve-hour days. In his happier days, Patrick wouldn't touch a beer during the work week. But he gradually started to binge on the weekends, beginning right when he woke up on Friday morning. By the time night fell, he would normally have consumed about fourteen to eighteen beers, sometimes more, all by himself. He started getting addicted to Hydrocodone as well. He said that the painkillers made him feel happy, so I didn't complain. He spent a lot of time trying to find people that had them. He also drank four to six large cans of energy drinks a day. Even with that, he would pass out and sleep in the garage. By the time Sunday night rolled around, he became more despondent, knowing that Monday was a work day. Gradually, he started missing work on Mondays.

After several weeks of this, his Supervisor mandated that he go to AA meetings. It made him realize the possibility of losing his job, and so as a result, he started a new sobriety phase, one that would last four years.

Sober, drunk, sober, drunk—it was a never-ending cycle that ineffectively covered the anger and emotional angst that he held inside. When I asked him about it, he would always say that it "wasn't me." He told me his dad never told him that he loved him, and that his childhood was fearful and sad. I kept trying to make it up to him with toys and trips, a superficial happiness that didn't last.

Like all addicts that go from one addiction to another, Patrick, in his total sobriety, had to find something seemingly innocuous to be addicted to. Along with the racing, and with the help of Anna, the study of crystals, aliens and conspiracy theories began to replace alcohol and drugs.

At first, I was completely sober with him. But he was a pain in the ass when he was sober. He was sad and withdrawn. The hardest thing for me is that he withdrew from me, acting as if I wasn't even there. He didn't want to do our surfing rituals anymore. He didn't pick up his skateboard at all. He was way more miserable sober than he was drunk.

I craved his affection, but I couldn't make him *want to* be affectionate to me. It's pathetic to even ask. Awkwardly asking him to do that doesn't make any of his efforts authentic. I didn't want a fake display of affection.

The only time we did anything together was when we went to AA meetings. For the longest time I tried to, but just couldn't hide the fact that I selfishly couldn't handle him being sober. The happy memories of us having fun together had vanished. The loneliest feeling is having someone you love there with you, but not *there.*

My loneliness became harder and harder to fight against. It wore me down, and I started taking anti-depressants to cope with it. But I had to focus on him, not me. *It was my mission to save him.*

I remembered a movie with a part about a guy that was in love with a hologram woman. In it, the guy comes home from a crazy workday dodging death, and is greeted by a beautiful hologram wearing lingerie saying, "Hello baby, relax and put your feet up. Let me get you a beer." Then she brings him a beer and starts to unzip his pants. She never complained or asked questions. I thought the hologram woman, in a man's eyes, was the epitome of a perfect wife. The guy is so in love with her because his needs were paramount and she didn't have any. Everything was all about him. Taking that unrealistic theory as desperate inspiration, I totally focused on Patrick and shoved my own needs way back into the darkness of ignorance. He was confused and thought I was acting weird. He was amused, but it didn't last. As his depression grew, he withdrew even more. His heart was so dark with pain, even the perfect woman couldn't save him.

I planned a trip back to a surf break in Nicaragua that we loved. But this time he hardly surfed, instead walked around by himself, watching frogs and toucans, monkeys and insects. I wasn't with him most of the time. *I* wanted to surf. When we were together, he hardly spoke. He wasn't mean to me. He knew it wore on me, and he always told me, "Honey, it's not your fault." I spent the vacation mostly alone, except for letting some local kids use my board and trying to teach them how to surf.

But I was on vacation, and now I wanted a drink, especially having to deal with Patrick's behavior and the memories of us having such an awesome time there before. I was trying to balance what I wanted to do, and how to be respectful to Patrick. He told me to go ahead because we were on vacation. Even though I felt guilty,

SOBER
TIMES

Heron Island

Nicaragua

Galapagos

Fiji

Costa Rica

43

at the same time I felt a weird kind of revenge. Like I needed to be happy too—not a victim of someone else's gloom.

Patrick locked himself into his own world of silence, barely speaking to anyone. The locals asked me what was wrong; he was so different than he was the last time they saw him. Looking into his eyes I could see his suffering. I would stare at him and wonder which horrible memory he was reliving. It was so sad to me, but I kept those emotions deep down so that I could try to enjoy my vacation, and not make his worse by talking about it.

I secretly wished he would start drinking again so that he could be happy. I started wishing it all the time, so that *we* could be happy and have fun together like we used to. I thought it was better to be drunk and happy sometimes than sober and miserable all the time.

I knew that I was selfish and not being supportive. I was just trying to find happiness in every way I could by myself. He was still kind to me, and he said he still loved me, but his expressions were dull and void of any passion. To know what you're missing is to remember what you had, and I no longer had him.

At home he still fixed anything that needed to be fixed, but other than that he would either be sleeping, racing or studying conspiracy theories. He demanded to be by himself, and pushed away anyone who tried to get close to him, sometimes even Anna.

I was probably part of his dysphoria. Maybe he needed me more than he knew how to tell me. You never really know how good things are until you find out how bad they can be, and you only see that in retrospect. I was too focused on working our way out of debt. I had displaced one ignorance for another, and it turned out to be deadly.

CHAPTER 8

Little did I know that very soon his depression would spiral into an even darker hell. Somewhere into the four years of sobriety, something serious at work pissed him off, and he started binging again. It irrevocably kick-started his already sensitive state of being to its final demise.

The trigger was his job as a Health Inspector. The State of California imposed new regulations on food facilities that turned Patrick and his colleagues from business-friendly advocates into "asshole enforcers", as one of his co-workers put it.

Before, he could go into an establishment, see filthy floors and tell the owner, "If you don't clean the floors, the rats will clean them for you", and then give them a reasonable amount of time to get rid of the rats and clean the place so that he wouldn't have to downgrade them.

But now, the new regulations took away all of the discretion that the Inspectors were trained for to help their establishments prosper. Now, walking in and seeing the same thing, the new System they were forced to use would instantly downgrade. There was no avenue to make an argument in defense of the robotic determination. The System didn't give a shit, didn't care about small businesses, nor those who ran the larger ones, it was just desperate to make money.

In addition, the new System now knew where the Inspectors were at all times. The Inspectors were given new work phones and laptops that were equipped with GPS tracking. Being an Inspector for fifteen years already, Patrick was infuriated that he and his co-workers were now being spied on. In Patrick's mind, the spying aspect went along with a lot of conspiracy theories he was now in full belief of, and his reaction was rebellious. His anger escalated. He bought aluminum-coated bags to keep his laptop and phone in. He came home angry every night. He started sleeping with loaded guns next to and under our bed.

The Inspectors that once worked with their establishments were now forced to work against them. Patrick now had to face the fallout at the places he inspected. The new rules left the owners angry, and some in despair. He saw how this hurt all those he worked so hard to help. There were many that he had a decade or more of working relationships with that he had grown to love and care about. Now he felt like he was betraying them. He took it very personally, and it devastated him. He was no longer their friend and advocate. Now he was forced to be their enemy.

At the same time, his best friend at work chose to retire early. She had always been his sounding board and his support, and was one of the very few people who really took the time to understand him. With her gone, he was even more distraught. It was more than he could bear. Patrick's distress erupted like a volcano with a vengeance.

He came home from work in tears every day for weeks, saying he did not want to go back. The job he once loved became the focus of a renewed anger that ignited the rage he held inside since childhood. In the hopelessness of a situation he couldn't change, he completely stopped skateboarding, surfing, racing, and everything else he once loved to do. All he did was sleep. He ignored everyone.

Again, he started missing work every Monday. This quickly started to extend into Tuesday, and then Wednesday. His supervisor put him into the AA meetings once again. This time, it was serious. He would lose his job if he didn't shape up.

One day I went to his work near the end of his work day because we were going to attend an AA meeting nearby right after. I went up to the room where the Inspector's office partitions were, and found him near his desk talking to one of his supervisors. She was a new hire, and came on the job after the new System was put into place. He introduced me to her, then they continued their conversation. As I stood nearby, I could hear his voice escalating. Everyone in the room started peeping over their partitions, and then stood up from their chairs. Patrick started yelling about how the new System had ruined the working relationships he'd spent years establishing, and that all the business-friendly faith was lost because of the dictatorial new policies. He was screaming, "I can't do this anymore, I can't keep hurting all these people. Fuck you! FUCK YOU! I HAVE TO GET OUT OF HERE!!!" I saw his supervisor back away as Patrick took a box and started throwing things in it from his desk. He became so violent that one of his co-workers grabbed him and tried to calm him down. At the same time, I could sense that all his co-workers were silently cheering. He was expressing everything they felt too. Patrick being Patrick—had the nerve to vehemently express it for everyone without any fear of the consequences. "Fuck you all!" he said as we walked out.

I was sure he was going to lose his job after that, but he didn't. He was one of their best inspectors. They placed him on an extended family leave. He was forced to see another psychiatrist, who prescribed a stronger Lexapro dose than the one he was already on. But Patrick was so distraught, and his despondence was worse than I had ever seen it.

Now that he didn't have to go to work, he started getting drunk and smoking pot all the time. He would sleep all day and night in our van in the garage, barely coming inside the house. It was horrible to see him this way, and there was nothing I could do to help him. He always demanded to be left alone.

When he wasn't sleeping, he was studying conspiracy theories. He became entrenched in research, staying up almost all night every night, with his ipad practically glued to his face. When he did decide to sleep in our bed instead of in the garage, it didn't seem to make a difference. He was so into the stuff on his ipad, it was if I wasn't even there in bed next to him anyway.

He began hoarding canned food in preparation for an apocalypse, and started collecting guns and ammunition. He even bought two gas masks. There were several 50-gallon bins of water and large slabs of plywood stashed in our garage. He believed there was going to be huge civil unrest, and that we would have to defend our house against attack.

The guns became an obsession. He bought a huge heavy duty safe to store them in. He toted the guns around the house and admired their beauty. He kept them immaculately clean. He went to Army/Navy stores and bought survival equipment and camoflauge gear. He frequently got drunk and dressed up in the camoflauge stuff with his guns and paraded around the house. This concerned me. It was really strange, kind of passively violent. I was afraid that he was seriously losing it.

Patrick did not ever live his life in moderation. It was either all or nothing. When something interested him, he gave it his full attention, studying everything about it that he could. I suppose this is what attracted me to him in the first place. In the beginning, it was *me* that was his obsession, and I loved the attention. I never had anyone treat me like that before, and that was wonderful in those first thirteen years of our marriage.

But I was gradually being replaced by guns and conspiracy theories. He spiraled into a disconnected world of his own, and it was out of my reach. I couldn't get him out of it, and I became increasingly concerned. He became so hypnotized by all this other stuff that we hadn't been having sex. Weeks would pass with him hardly looking at me, and hardly ever speaking to me. I started feeling more isolated than ever. The conspiracy theories may or may not be true, I thought. I said to him, "Even if this stuff is true, we can't change any of it. But we *can* change *us! What about us? Aren't WE more important?"* I wanted him to see that. I needed him to see that. "Hello! *I Need You! I want my husband back!"*

I longed for the quiet mornings we would wake up super early and surf in peace with only the sound of the waves breaking. To try to comfort myself, I continued to go on my own. It helped in a calming way, but at the same time it made me miss him. Even the waves couldn't wash away the feeling that I was slowly losing him.

Patrick had put up an impenetrable barrier and only his demons had entrance rights. When I tried to talk to him, he would say, "Honey, it isn't you, it's not your fault" and "I have to deal with my demons." But I was living in fear of what he might do, and didn't want him to be alone, especially with all the guns.

One morning I woke up next to Patrick and saw a loaded revolver on the headboard shelf a few inches away from his head. He was in another drunken oblivion, not even moving when I woke up. I freaked out. I took the gun and ran downstairs to get it away from him. My reaction was purely impulsive and idiotic. I was not familiar with the gun, and I was hoping to disarm it. As I was handling it, I barely touched the trigger and ended up firing a bullet through the outer wall of our house. I was shaking, and shocked at my stupidity. I immediately went outside to see if I could find the bullet, or if I could hear screaming because I had just killed somebody. There was a hole about a foot in diameter through the outer wall of our house. I was very lucky that the bullet did not hit anyone or anything that someone owned. I was surprised that no one called the cops. If I had been pointing the gun in any other direction, I easily could have shot a neighbor, my dog Frito (who at the time was sitting just a few feet away from me), or myself.

The sound woke Patrick and he stumbled downstairs, still drunk, telling me what a "stupid bitch" I was, over and over again. I didn't argue with him, because this ranks at the top of the list of one of the stupidest things I had ever done.

I had increasing fear that he was suicidal. I constantly checked on him while he was in the garage. I was terribly worried and distracted from my work. It seemed like there was no joy left in him at all, about anything.

I wanted so badly for him to be happy again. I wished for it to be like before when he would tell me he loved me. But he was a different person then. Now I am living with his demons.

I lived alone in our home, even with him there. I was forced in silence to my own world. I still did everything I could to make life comfortable for him, like making sure his towels were warm, his clothes washed and folded, the house quiet and in order; mostly trying to stay upbeat for him. That became harder and harder to do.

I hated watching him sleep. He slept more than I had ever seen anyone sleep. He was asleep more hours than he was awake, and when he was awake, all he did was study conspiracy theories. All of this crowded out our time together. He was there, but somewhere else. The resentment was building inside me. I had to handle all of the bills and work extra hard. I compartmentalized things so that I didn't stay angry. It was increasingly harder to pay down the credit card debt from all of our vacations when I was the only one working. I began to hate that he wasn't helping me and that he didn't seem to care. I hated that he didn't have any regard for my needs at all, and what our marriage needed to survive.

ARE YOU AN ALCOHOLIC?

The list of questions which follows has helped a lot of people find where they stood with booze. But remember, you are the only one who can say if you have a problem or not. Even if you've been told you do, the important thing is that you decide for yourself. All we ask is that you try to be honest.

		Yes	No
1.	Did you lose time from work due to drinking?	(X)	( )
2.	Did drinking make your home life unhappy	(X)	( )
3.	Did you drink because you were shy with people?	(X)	( )
4.	Has drinking affected your reputation?	(X)	( )
5.	Have you gotten into trouble with money because of your drinking?	(X)	( )
6.	Did you associate with people you didn't respect and hang out in places you didn't want to be in when drinking?	(X)	( )
7.	Did your drinking make you careless of your family's welfare?	(X)	( )
8.	Has your drinking decreased you ambition?	(X)	( )
9.	Did you want a drink "the morning after?"	(X)	( )
10.	Did you have a hard time sleeping because of your drinking?	(X)	( )
11.	Has your ability to work decreased since drinking?	(X)	( )
12.	Did drinking get you into trouble on the job or in business?	(X)	( )
13.	Did you drink to escape from problems or worries?	(X)	( )
14.	Did you drink alone?	(X)	( )
15.	Have you ever had a complete loss of memory as a result of drinking?	(X)	( )
16.	Has a doctor ever treated you for drinking?	(X)	( )
17.	Did you drink to build up self-confidence?	(X)	( )
18.	Have you ever been arrested, locked up or hospitalized on account of your drinking?	(X)	( )
19.	Have you ever felt guilty after drinking?	(X)	( )
20.	Did you have to have a drink at a certain time each day?	( )	(X)

If you answered "yes" to three or more questions, you may be an alcoholic. But remember, we in A.A. follow this program voluntarily. No one forces us to admit we are alcoholics. No one forces us to stay sober in A.A. We do it because we like what A.A. has to offer

I worked harder to focus on reality. And the reality was at that time we were over $70,000 in credit card debt. I was frustrated, because he had spent most of his paychecks on stuff we didn't need. But I didn't say anything at the time, because I knew material things made him (temporarily) happy.

I was working so hard, that Patrick would say that every time he saw me, my head was turned to the computer. The debt nagged at me and I couldn't relax. I told him I was working so hard because I wanted to buy him nice things and still be able to go on our trips.

To me, Patrick's happiness was paramount. I had a misguided view that his happiness depended on how much money I made so that he could have more *stuff*. The paradox was that the time it took to make the money took away the time to spend it.

I ended up telling him about the debt, and we cut back on our trips, but it was impossible to do that entirely. The first thing on my mind was saving him, and compared to that, the debt didn't matter.

I thought of one thing that might snap him out of it. I spent a lot of money to take him to to a rainforest at a remote surf break on the southern Pacific side of Costa Rica that he always wanted to visit. Some of the light came back into his eyes when I told him, and in the preparation to go there, he almost seemed excited.

It was deep in the jungle and very hard to get to. There were hours of driving through muddy roads and giant puddles that looked impassable. On the way there, we had our driver stop at a small store. Patrick came out with five large bottles of Cacique Guaro, which is a Costa Rican liquor distilled from sugar cane. I thought, "do we really need *all* that?"

Once we got to our casita, he stayed inside the majority of all the ten days we were there, laying in bed sleeping, and drinking all day long until he passed out. I could not believe that he did not want to surf, especially here, at this incredible spot. Before the week was over he drank all five bottles of Cacique. I surfed alone, and looked for frogs alone. I tried to keep a positive mind so that I didn't ruin my own vacation, and kept hoping that he would come around and start enjoying his.

The signs were all there that it would probably be our last. If being in this rainforest he had always dreamed of—full of hundreds of species of frogs, giant insects, majestic butterflies, leaves larger than the roof of our house, and a super fun point break at the bottom of the trail didn't make him happy, nothing would.

The days passed in solitude. With my first husband as one who rarely spoke, I had learned to interpret love mostly by the physical expression of it. And now, Patrick and I hadn't had sex for almost a year. I told him that made me feel like he didn't love me anymore. He told me he still did, and it's not my fault.

CHAPTER 9

I came home one day after doing an errand for work and found Patrick in the garage, sobbing uncontrollably. I grabbed him and held him tight, trying to hold myself back from panicking. He was shaking while he said, "Do you know what I just did?" I let go of him, stood back, and said "OMG! What? What happened!?"

He told me he went inside the van with one of his revolvers, put a bullet in the chamber, and spun it. He then put the gun inside his mouth. He pulled the trigger—*click*—nothing happened. I was horrified. He said he was overcome by something inside him that told him he should kill himself. The demons he was battling within him almost got their way. The bullet that would have blown his brains out was in the very next chamber.

I had never seen Patrick like this before. There was no way I could console him, because I was shaking and crying too. I was freaking out so I called his sister. He objected, but I told him I had to, because if I didn't call her I would call 911 instead. With that choice he said, "Okay call her then. Just don't call my parents!" Since his sister was a retired police officer, she was trained in how to handle things like this. She came over promptly and took him to her house, where he stayed overnight.

The next day when he came home his agitation had subsided, but he was very quiet and withdrawn. He said he was exhausted. I told his sister to take the revolver and keep it. I told Patrick I wanted her to take *all* of his guns but he refused.

I didn't know the combination to the safe. He told me once and I learned the sequence of opening it but now I only remembered two of the numbers. You had to use a key first and I had no clue where that was. I wish I had written down the numbers, but if I didn't have the key that wouldn't matter anyway. When I asked him for the combination and where he kept the key, he immediately said, "No! You had your chance."

He begged me to not ever tell his mom and dad about his suicide attempt, because he didn't want them around. Ultimately I think he just didn't want to witness their denial anymore.

It was his sister that told them. And Patrick was right. They both looked the other way. I couldn't believe it. I thought they should be as horrified as I was, and come over right away to be with him. Instead, Patrick's mom called, and he spoke to her pretending that he was okay.

He told me, "You know what's weird? My dad is the one that beat me up all the time—but I love the guy. I love him so much. My mom, she didn't protect us." I was surprised that he said that because I always witnessed his mom as gentle and loving, hardly ever raising her voice. She had a very calming way about her. She balanced the aggression in the family. I really believe if she hadn't been this way Patrick and his brother and sisters would have had much less of a chance of doing so well in life. They all turned out to be exemplary employees and high-achievers. They were all top performers in their professions. They were all totally cool to everybody and had big hearts just like their father. They also had their mother's softness. I think that without their mother's gentle balance, their lives could have been a lot worse.

After that suicide episode I should have never left his side. But he demanded to be alone. I was damned if I did, and damned if I didn't.

CHAPTER 10

I encouraged Patrick to go back to work because I thought he might feel better by concentrating on other things. With trepidation, he called his boss a few days after. She was glad to hear from him and welcomed him back without hesitation. He even admitted as fucked up as the protocol at work was, he actually did miss work and his office buddies.

Patrick started hanging out more with our neighbor Anna. She was at our house a lot because she didn't work, and it didn't seem like she wanted to. He spent a lot of time with her discussing spirituality, and it seemed to be a good distraction for him. She was looking out for him too. They were pretty close. That was okay with me because she was always smiling and happy. She was also very intuitive. I would find out things from her that Patrick had not told me. I had to ask her how he was doing, since he hardly spoke to me.

He seemed to start feeling better. With inspiration from Anna, he became obsessed with meditation, self-healing, and making necklaces. He went to the bead store and spent thousands of dollars on semi-precious gemstones. I kept my mouth shut about how much he was spending. It was more important that he take care of himself, and if this made his happy, his life was worth the debt. Fuck the credit cards.

I looked for ways to find new bonds with Patrick, so I started asking him about his conspiracy theory beliefs. This enabled us to talk more. But the conspiracy theories inspired fear and mistrust. I could see how one could become paranoid and worried. Some of them sounded absolutely insane, and they were hard for me to believe, but he believed them. I listened and tried hard not to argue.

I desperately wanted us to hang out together again. I persuaded him to go with me to look for frogs. We managed to surf together sometimes. One day we went on a long hike with some of his friends from work. We hardly walked together. He was distant and weird, mostly walking by himself. When I tried to walk with him, he said he just wanted to be by himself. I thought we were being rude to his friends, so I walked with them mostly. His work friends were asking me if he was okay, and I told them that 'he was trying.'

I tried to tell Patrick what I needed in the most non-accusational and non-threatening way I could, but he didn't seem to want to listen. I told him I constantly needed to know that he loved me, either by saying it, but mostly by *showing* it. I told him I was worried because we hadn't had sex for over a year. I thought that should be a pretty simple request because he's a guy. But he interpreted this as though I was complaining, and he responded by complaining. I had to forget about it and live in denial to get through each day.

The new policies at work still upset him, but he and his colleagues found ways to work around them. Still, he would come home at 6 pm and go right back to the garage. A lot of times he wouldn't even eat dinner. I barely got to talk to him. He would just ignore me. He had also stopped taking his Lexapro. He said, "Fuck this, it doesn't work." I told him, "You're not supposed to quit all at once, that's going to screw you up more! Go back to the psychiatrist!" He said, "Fuck them, they don't give a fuck about me."

As the months passed, I could see our respect for each other diminishing. I observed in other couples that once they lost respect for one another, they never gained it back, and ended up divorcing. I didn't see myself ever divorcing Patrick. That would be my failure in trying to fix him. I never wanted to give up trying. We had so many good times together, and I wanted them back. I wanted *him* back.

Patrick was drowning in a pool of misery, and I was hopeless in all my attempts to rescue him. Anna helped keep his head above water. He seemed a little happier when he was with her. I wanted him to be around whatever positive reinforcement there was. She was like a lifeguard. I was able to work with less worry when she was with him. She had a calming way of talking to him, and she even made him laugh sometimes.

I was very busy trying to catch up on our debt. Watching him sleep was not productive for me, and left me no choice but to work. When Anna was around, my guilt was alleviated for not spending time watching Patrick. He would usually wake up when she came over. They would go hang out, and since she was with him, I would go back inside and work.

CHAPTER 11

The incessant energy to put Patrick first and focus on his happiness wore me down little by little, days turning into months that turned into years. I left myself behind somewhere in all that effort. The sacrifice I was too afraid to admit started talking out loud, before I had time to analyze the potential consequences.

There was a guy I always saw at the gym that was very good-looking. One day he walked by me while I was using the crunch machine, and before I could stop myself, I heard myself saying, "I think you're cute." In horror, I thought, OMG, did I just say that?

He smiled and said, "You're cute too." From that point on, every time I saw him at the gym we would talk. When he asked me if I wanted to hang out, I told him I was married. He said, "Happily?" I hesitantly responded by saying my marriage was in a rough spot. I asked him if he was married, and he told me he wasn't.

He kept asking me over and over again to hang out, and finally my loneliness got the best of me. I broke down and went on a lunch date with him.

We started hanging out almost every day. I enjoyed the company and the attention. I realized I was starting to feel happy again, with a new energy that was positive rather than negative. I looked forward to the next time I could see him.

My needs were impossible to ignore once I let my defenses down. Weeks later, when he came on to me, I didn't make him stop. Too quickly I found myself in an affair, enveloped in the shame and guilt that went along with it.

I couldn't handle the dreadful feelings I had every time I woke up and realized my actions were not a bad dream I just had. Facing up to the horrible truth of reality, I told him I did not want to see him anymore.

This made me even more desperate to get my marriage to work again. I told Patrick I wanted to go to the place where he proposed to me. He said okay, and we went. But he was distant and strange. I hugged him tight and he hugged me loosely for just a moment, then let go. He stood back and said, "What's gotten into you?" I said, "What has gotten into *YOU?* You don't seem like you even *like* me anymore."

I asked him if we could go to marriage counseling. He told me flat out, "No. It's a fucking waste of time." I started to cry, and told him I didn't understand what had happened to us. He said, "Honey, it's not you. I just have to deal with my demons. That's why we don't need to go to marriage counseling. It's me that has problems."

I remembered the response I got when I play-acted like the hologram woman so I started countering his rejection by smothering him with affection—even with knowing I likely wouldn't get it in return. I knew that the hologram woman ideal wasn't real, but at this point I was so desperate for any kind of positive response from him, and this was the most pathetic attempt.

As I feared, he didn't respond the way I wanted him to. He waved his arm at me as if to protect himself from outside intrusion, saying either "Not now", or "Don't." I was coming to a point where I didn't know what else I could do. Patrick had shut the door on me. Even though my energy was running at an all time low, I was determined not to give up trying to do anything I could do to make him happy.

It was hard for me not to think about the affair, especially when my makeshift lover kept calling and texting me. I let almost three weeks go by, completely ignoring him. I instead focused on distracting myself with work. I kept my phone away from me where I would not be tempted to look at it. I also surfed alot and changed my gym schedule so I wouldn't run into him.

Ignoring him didn't last very long. Loneliness was creeping in again, despite my efforts to keep it away. One day I felt really down and I texted back. Less than an hour later our reunion was hotter than ever. In a sick way I felt it was a kind of revenge. What about *me?* I had been working my ass off and trying to pay all the bills. I felt unappreciated and irrelevant. I was angry and hurt inside. I was longing for the old Patrick. But now his demons had control over him, and that was a formidable battle I couldn't win.

The affair divided me two different entities that fought against one another. My body was in complete obstinance to the anguish of my soul. I was imprisoned in a selfish body that had been pulled into evil with a pretty face. Spellbound by my lover's charismatic hypnosis, I disconnected with all of my true feelings. My false happiness was a yin and yang of my own self-loathing. I saw myself like I was in an audience watching another actor's performance and not my own. To my horror this *was me*, living this madness, and now it was too late to change the script.

I knew I was using my lover as a utility to make up for what I needed from Patrick, the man I *really* loved. So many times I wanted to run away from this evil as far as I could. But the incessant magnet of loneliness kept enchanting me back to my sugar-coated misery. I hated myself.

CHAPTER 12

The truth hurt too much, so I chose to let bullshit reign. The bullshit said: "Wait. Not yet. Save your emotional energy. You don't need to tell him about the affair right now. Why ruin everything faster?" I had an obscure and intangible wish that something else would happen where the truth could be revealed in a less painful way.

Uh huh. *As if.* As it happens, I wouldn't have to verbally explain, the truth would be fatally exposed in plain sight. And it was the dreaded scenario I never wanted to come true. Somehow though, I knew it would happen, and with knowing that—why did I engage in this? My body-soul duality had always confounded me.

I knew this day would come. It wasn't a matter of *if*, it was a matter of *when*. It was 2:30 on Monday afternoon. My lover and I were upstairs and had just finished a sex session—when we heard the front door open.

Oh shit—OMG—Patrick had come home from work early—this can't be happening! I never saw my boyfriend move so fast. He jumped up, got dressed and pathetically looked for a place to hide. I went down the stairs as I was putting on my clothes and said that I had just been in the shower. But there was no way I could hide what I had been doing. And I am a really shitty liar.

The fantasy world I had been in quickly closed in around me, spiraling my thoughts into chaos. I couldn't speak. I couldn't move. My senses all grayed out. There was no Command Z—the *undo* buttons just weren't there.

Patrick looked around really fast and said, "I know someone's here. Who's here? What is going on? Is your boyfriend here?" He stormed upstairs, going through every closet, and then found my lover trembling with humility in the shower, in dread of knowing he couldn't possibly explain his way out of this. Patrick said, "I knew it! Get Out. GET OUT! GET THE FUCK OUT OF HERE BEFORE I FUCKING KILL YOU!"

Patrick told me, "You too!—*Now*! You fucking whore! I knew it! YOU FUCKING WHORE!!!"

I felt I was in two levels of consciousness, simultaneosly. All of my evils finally caught up with me. Even with knowing that this day would come, it couldn't have fully prepared me for the reality of how I would feel when it actually happened. The rest of the week was a blur. I was numb with feelings I didn't have words for. I was smothered in so much shame that I literally wanted to die.

I drove to my friend Wendy's house like I was in auto-pilot. I didn't have to think. I was too numb to panic. I caused this to happen. It's all my fault.

Patrick spent the rest of that day and on into the night with two of his best friends at our house, drinking himself into oblivion. At 3 in the morning, he called me and said, "You can come over in the morning and get your stuff. I threw it outside."

I got there at dawn. The upstairs bedroom window screen was ripped open, and a lot of my stuff laid broken and wet from the dew on the ground below. It was a big embarrassing mess. I was still sleepwalking like I was living in a bad dream.

I felt like I was separate from my body, which automatically did what it had to do on its own. My disgraced soul had to detach in order for my body to function.

After unloading the car full of my stuff from the first trip to

Wendy's, I went back home for more stuff, and saw Patrick sitting on the bench in front of our house, very sad, with his head down. He never looked up at me. Seeing him this way was as bad as seeing him after he had had the revolver in his mouth. I don't think I had ever felt so horrible in all my life. I wished I could die right there. There was nothing I could say to redeem myself. How could I do this to the man I love more than anything, that I knew suffered so much?

I was so humiliated. I just wanted to get my stuff out of public view as fast as I could, and I tried not to think emotionally. I gathered as much as I could fit into the car back and forth each time. It took five trips. My hands and fingers were raw and my body ached. For a week, the neighbors watched a true-to-life drama unfolding in front of our house. My embarrassment and shame were displayed like a gigantic neon sign spelling WHORE in front of the whole world. People probably filmed and uploaded this mess of my life on YouTube. I didn't want to know. I never felt so ashamed.

I turned Wendy's house into a complete disaster. On the fourth trip back, Patrick was no longer sitting on the bench silent, but was now extremely agitated. He was forcefully throwing dresser drawers out of the bedroom window above, almost as if he was trying to hit me. He was repeatedly yelling out, "My wife is a fucking whore! You LOWLIFE SLUT-CUNT-WHORE!" I wasn't sure if he was trying to aim these objects at me or not. But now he was out of control, and I didn't feel safe.

I went back to Wendy's and called the local sheriffs office. I told them that I had been kicked out of my house by my husband because of the affair, and that he owned a lot of guns. They asked me if Patrick had threatened me physically in any way. I told them no, he never threatened to harm me ever, but that I was concerned that he may be suicidal. I described his aggressive behavior that I had just witnessed, and that I feared for his safety,

EXCERPT FROM PERT REPORT:

DEPUTY'S OBSERVATIONS AND ACTIONS continued:

I had Deputy (4)   contact   (Patrick Sharp) by phone prior to going to the home.   He was home with a friend and was okay with us all coming to the house. Deputy (4)   and I contacted (Patrick) and his friend Rob, outside the home, on the green-belt. There was a large amount of personal property items on the grass, outside the house.   (Mrs. Sharp) stayed in her car, out of sight, with another Deputy. I introduced myself to (Patrick) and walked him away from the house, to a location where he was out of sight of (Mrs. Sharp). Once away from the house, (Mrs. Sharp) was allowed to obtain her property. (Patrick Sharp) told me the following:

Statements of   (Patrick Sharp) :

Upon initial contact, (Patrick) said he did not have any guns and even if he did, I could not take them When I told (Patrick) I worked with a psychiatric therapist, he became upset and said "I don't want to speak to any fucking therapist. I have nothing to say. They don't help." He said he would talk with me. (Patrick) said he had come home in the evening/night and found another man in his shower.   (Mrs. Sharp) was home. He had suspected she was cheating for some time. He was very upset and did not think it was fair to make him leave his home, when he had done nothing wrong. (Patrick) said if he had a gun, he could have shot the guy in the kneecaps, right there. He said he didn't, because he was not that type of person. He did not want to hurt anyone. He was extremely upset and loved his wife. (Patrick) was extremely upset and had been drinking heavily. When I talked with him about the concerns of his guns, he told me he would never do anything stupid, he would not hurt himself. He said he couldn't do that, because it wasn't fair to other people. He told me several times he was fine and would not do anything to himself.

DEPUTY'S OBSERVATIONS AND ACTIONS continued:

After about 20-25 minutes, Deputy (4) told me (Mrs. Sharp) was done at the home. I walked back to the house with (Patrick). He joked with me about him being older than me and in better shape. I spoke with Rob, with (Patrick) present. Rob said he would stay with (Patrick) and watch him. I provided (Patrick) a PERT Resource Pamphlet with my name and phone number on it. I told him to call me if he needed someone to talk with. He said he would and that he would be okay.

65

and mine.

After giving them a more detailed description of Patrick's recent behavior, I asked for a sheriff's officer to escort me back to my house so that I could get the rest of my things. An hour and a half later, I arrived with one of the local deputies, who had brought with him a PERT (Psychiatric Emergency Response Team) Officer.

As one of the deputies stood nearby, I got the rest of my things. Patrick didn't talk to me nor even look at me at all. I could see the PERT officer in a conversation with him across the grass. Patrick looked as if he had settled down. They talked for about fifteen minutes.

That night was my third sleepless night on a pile of clothes at Wendy's house. Patrick called me at 3:15 am. At first I didn't get the phone. I didn't want to keep hearing what a lowlife whore I was.

But he wouldn't stop calling. I finally picked up. Patrick said, "Honey please come home. Please come home now. I forgive you. Please come home. This is my fault, it's my fault that this happened." I could tell he hadn't stopped drinking. I said, "Do you really mean it, are you sure? Is this a trick?" He emphatically said, "No, I really mean it. Please come home now, I love you, I want you here with me, just come back!"

After we hung up I went home. I couldn't find my shoes at Wendy's, so I walked barefoot on the dewy pavement. Everything felt so weird. I walked in the door, and Patrick came up and hugged me. We both started crying. The house inside was such a mess that it was unrecognizable. We were both exhausted and went up to our bedroom. We laid on a top of a pile of random stuff, hugging and crying. I was still stunned, and felt like I was in a weird dream where nothing made sense.

I told him that the only reason I had the affair was because he had been totally ignoring me for way too long. Through alot of tears, he said he was so, so sorry, then screamed out: "HOW COULD YOU DO THIS TO ME!!!" I had been crying so hard that my throat was raw. I told him I was selfish, and that I had never felt worse about anything I'd ever done before in my life.

We tried to sleep but couldn't, even though neither of us had slept for days. We agonized about how we hurt each other, even though the apologies were now too late. The remorse that was cutting through me made me feel like I was about to die. And I deserved it.

As we laid there talking, Patrick rewound the history of his life, playing it back to me so vividly, that I felt as if I was watching his life in real time.

He cried in guilt about the wrongs he had done to others in the past, wishing he could tell them all at this very moment how sorry he was. He talked about his first girlfriend, and his relationships all the way up to his life with me. He was unforgiving of himself, remembering how he'd hurt so many people. He also talked about the wrongs others had done to him, that he had struggled his whole life trying to forget. I often wondered why people use the phrase "forgive and forget." I always thought that forgiving was an uncommon blessing of divine intervention, and that forgetting was due to getting so old you can't remember why you should forgive or be forgiven in the first place.

I emphasized to Patrick the many people we knew that recognized his sensitive and beautiful soul, and that loved him very much in the best way they knew how. I told him how much I loved his impulsive nature that acted on spontaneous whims that either ended up in disaster or as the best of times. He was the most fun and interesting person to be with. I told him how badly I wanted him to be happy again, how I wished he could dump the conspiracy theories and have fun again, without fearing the end was just around the corner. I did not expect that the end of *him* was.

The following day we woke up before dawn and got busy trying to put everything back the way it was. Patrick fixed the furniture that he had thrown out of the window a few days before.

It was just getting dark, when Patrick said he was hungry. He went to Ralph's. He came back with some beer and a container of cut up fruit. I was still upstairs putting things in place, when I heard him say, "Honey come here!" I went down to the kitchen, and saw him standing next to the sink eating the fruit. He was holding a gigantic strawberry on his fork and had just taken a bite. As I was coming down the stairs I heard him say, "Omg— honey, this is the *best* thing I have *ever* tasted!"

Then he said, "Here—this is so good, that I want *you* to have it." I said, "No, if it's that good, I want *you* to have it." He looked at me with so much love, I felt like I was seeing him again in those years long ago when he was happy. I will never forget the way he looked at me right then.

He took the fork and put it to my mouth and insisted that I eat the rest of the strawberry. To me, it tasted like any other strawberry, so I wasn't sure at the time why he made such a big deal about it.

The next morning I would find out that it would be the last thing he was ever going to eat. And it would be the last time I would ever see that look in his eyes.

Late into the night, we were too exhausted to work anymore. He ran out of alcohol. Then he said he couldn't find his wallet, and asked if I would go get him some vodka. I refused. When he wasn't looking, I hid my wallet, which wasn't hard amongst all the mess still around. But while I was in the shower, he found it.

When I came out of the shower, he was gone. Then I looked over and saw my open wallet on the countertop. I was horrified that he even thought he was okay enough to drive. The lure of the liquid demons enticed him with the power that deceived him into thinking he could do *anything*.

Fifteen minutes later, he came home carrying a plastic 1.75 liter of cheap vodka. He told me, "You're not going to believe this, but when I pulled into the parking space at the liquor store, a cop car drove up and parked right next to me. I was sure he had been following me. He walked right behind me into the store, and I went in acting like I didn't notice him, but I was freaked out thinking he was waiting to give me a DUI. But then I turned around and saw the cop go behind the counter, talking and laughing with the guy that worked there. I walked up to the counter and paid for the vodka, and couldn't believe that the cop didn't pay attention to how drunk I was. I couldn't believe he let me walk out of there and get into the car and drive away. I mean, the dude was fuckin' so close I was sure he could smell me! Man, I lucked out!"

At the time, I thought he was very lucky indeed. But I didn't know that no sooner than the next morning I would wish that that ignorant sheriff would have noticed how drunk he was, and follow him in his car long enough to arrest him.

CHAPTER 13

Patrick took the vodka bottle he just bought, ripped off the top and began guzzling it, without even taking the time to pour it into a glass.

A short time later when we went to bed and tried to sleep, he told me to call my boyfriend right then and there. I found my phone and rang him several times, but he didn't pick up. It was almost midnight. I said to Patrick that I would call him when I knew he would be awake. Patrick started crying again, and said, "I can't believe you did this, HOW COULD YOU DO THIS TO ME?" It was a painful replay of the night before. I told him that I was for sure going to end the affair in the morning. I kept telling him that I loved him so much, and that I had *never been more sorry about anything I had ever done.* After hashing out the agony all over again, we both were exhausted, and fell asleep. About an hour later he woke up and started talking about going to Sulawesi as soon as possible. I was glad that he had changed the subject, and it made me feel secure about not losing him. We made love, and fell asleep.

I woke up just before 9 am and went down to the kitchen to make some tea. Patrick was still asleep. The water had just begun to boil, and as I was pouring it into my cup, I saw Patrick coming down the stairs, naked, holding the shotgun that he kept under the bed. By the look on his face and his aggressive motions, I knew that the tightly wound spool of anger he held within was quickly unraveling, and was about to spin out of control.

It took me by surprise—I really believed we were in the process of working things out. But Patrick's unpredictable behavior swung from one extreme to the other. There was never any moderation.

I immediately picked up the phone and pushed 9-1... As I pushed the last 1, Patrick said, "If you call 911, *I'm going to do it!*" I immediately hung up the phone. To my horror, Patrick got on his knees in the kitchen with the shotgun under his chin.

I heard myself shouting, "YOU CAN'T DO IT—THE GUN IS JAMMED!" I had no idea how I knew that. There was no earthly way I could have known that. I did not know how to use that gun. I had never even touched it. The words just came out, blantantly resolute. But I was right. The gun *WAS* jammed!

Patrick cussed over and over again, shaking the shotgun and moving its parts, trying to do whatever to fix it. Then he went outside in our backyard, got on his knees with the shotgun under his chin, and tried again. It still didn't work. He paid no attention to me or anything else around him. With me *somehow knowing* that the gun was jammed, I burst into action.

The first thing was my dogs. I put Frito in his crate under the stairs, where I knew he felt safe. Then I carried Emo outside to the garage, where he liked to hang out inside the van. As I was running toward the garage with Emo, I saw our neighbor Tim, who was one of Patrick's best friends. Without even saying hi, I rushed by close to him and said, "Patrick's got the shotgun and he's in the backyard trying to kill himself!" Without another word, Tim ran to our house.

I didn't know that even though I had hung up, that the 9-1-1 call would actually go through. The police were there in less than five minutes. After I secured Emo in the garage, I ran back to my house, and passed a sheriff decked out in a bulletproof vest, carrying an AR-15. He had a fierce look in his eyes, staring straight ahead, running past me like he was a soldier approaching combat. After I saw the crazed demeanor of that deputy, I knew that Patrick wouldn't stand a chance.

When I approached the house, I heard Patrick saying to Tim, "Get the fuck out of here! GET THE FUCK OUT!" Tim was one of Patrick's best friends. I knew he wouldn't shoot him, nor would he shoot me, or anyone else. He just wanted to end his own suffering. I did not fear for anyone else's life except Patrick's.

Patrick gave up on the shotgun, and came back into the house to open the safe. For some weird reason, he couldn't open it. I couldn't believe that, because he knew the entire sequence by heart. I saw him opening it and locking it back up by memory all the time without any problems. But this time he couldn't get it right. What had always worked before, somehow this time just *didn't*.

I heard him shouting, "Fuck! Fuck!! FUCK!!!" He was moving aggressively, his body taken over by that thing inside himself that he hated, the evil thing he fought against his entire life, the thing that relentlessly tortured him and was always stealing his joy. Today, he was going to give up and let it win.

CHAPTER 14

We both saw a cop run by our front door. It looked like the same guy than ran past me before. He never paused to try to speak to us. I looked outside the screen door, and saw another deputy running across the grass further away. It looked like they were positioning themselves for a shootout or something. Everything was happening so fast.

Patrick pulled on some shorts, grabbed the 3/4 full plastic vodka bottle from the kitchen counter, and with the shotgun in his other hand, resolutely walked toward the front door. I was frantic. I yelled, "NOOOO!!!! DON'T DO THIS - DON'T GO OUT THERE!!! STAY WITH ME!!!" But his mind was already made up. Right as he got to the front door, he turned his head slightly and said, "If I can't do it, I'm going to get them to do it for me. See you in the next life." That was the last audible thing he said to me.

I was stunned by Patrick's temerarious and unwavering resolve. He walked outside about fifty feet away from our front door—the entire time in the position of holding his arms straight out beside him in the form of a cross. I followed him. In his right hand he held the shotgun by its middle section, with the barrel pointing up to the sky. In his left hand he held the plastic vodka bottle by its handle. He stopped and stood completely still, facing two deputies that were aiming their guns at him. One of them was yelling, "Drop your weapon!" Patrick was motionless. I really don't think he thought they would actually shoot him.

I had followed him, until I heard Deputy 1 yell at me to get back. I stopped in the grass about twenty feet away from Patrick.

What I saw next looked like a military-style assault on Patrick, done without consideration for his mental state and without any reverence for human life.

There were no words of intervention, like "You don't have to do this, let us help you" or whatever proper things that should have been said. Patrick wasn't pointing the weapon at anyone, and he wasn't in any position that would indicate he was going to. He remained standing motionless, like a sacrificial cross.

Deputy 1 yelled at me to get back, and then began yelling at Patrick to drop his weapon. He shouted, "DROP YOUR WEAPON, DROP YOUR WEAPON!" two times in quick succession. I thought I heard Patrick say in a calm voice, "Shoot me."

Patrick let the vodka bottle fall from his left hand, with his arms still straight out beside him. Before it even hit the ground, Deputy 1 began shooting. Boom, boom, (slight pause) boom, boom. One of the shots had grazed Patrick and made him lose his balance, and the next shot struck him fatally while he was stumbling from the first.

I saw Patrick stagger, then spin around 180°, falling straight down on his face in the opposite direction. In the process of doing that he had dropped the shotgun, but now that was of no consequence. I saw a huge gaping hole gushing blood out of Patrick's left side, about six inches underneath his armpit.

He was lying face-down, trying to breathe. I saw his back heaving, as thick blood gushed from his side. He struggled to raise his head from the grass. As he did, I saw that he took great effort to mouth the words, "I Love You" to me, without the breath to say them audibly. Right after that, his face fell down into the grass.

I screamed: "YOU KILLED HIM!!! WHY DID YOU KILL HIM?!! DO YOU KILL SOMEBODY JUST BECAUSE THEY

ARE DEPRESSED?!!!" I remember yelling that several times, while two deputies came up from behind me, and roughly grabbed both of my arms from underneath and dragged me away from Patrick. They wouldn't let me be with him.

I was hysterical. Every sound dulled around me, and my entire body went numb. I was screaming, and sobbing so hard I couldn't breathe. It was like this wasn't really happening to me. Everything seemed to be in slow motion. It was like I was standing outside my own body watching this all happen. Did I really just see *my husband* get murdered before my eyes?

I couldn't believe what I just saw. There was no way I could understand how that deputy could just kill him, especially in the sacrificial way Patrick was standing. I couldn't justify it, no matter how hard I tried. I could see why the deputy would maybe shoot Patrick if he were in the position to be able to point a gun at him. But he *never* was.

The neighbors all came outside. I felt paralyzed. I just witnessed an inhumane execution; something that didn't need to happen. Everything felt wrong. I couldn't speak. I could not believe how my husband's life was taken away because some delusional moron with a badge felt like using him for target practice.

Another deputy took my arm and put me into the back of a sheriff SUV. They left me there for several minutes, with the doors locked and the windows rolled up all the way. It was really hot, and I couldn't breathe. Because I was crying so hard, I began hyperventalating. I started pound on the window and yell through the dark glass at anyone outside that could maybe hear me, to get someone to open a window. Finally one of my neighbors heard me, and a deputy came over and opened the window partway. A few minutes after that, I was being driven to the sheriff station, without shoes, without my phone, without underwear, in a mini skirt and t-shirt. I asked to be able to get my phone and change clothes but I wasn't allowed back into my house. Why?

It was a little after 10 that morning. I saw them recording me while they were driving me to the sheriff station. I was crying hysterically. No one in a uniform seemed to have any regard about how I was feeling about what I had just seen. There was never a grief counselor provided to me.

I witnessed with my own eyes without a doubt two deputies aiming their guns at Patrick. Deputy 2 had stated in his deposition that he didn't see anything. But *I saw him see it*. I know for certain that myself and Deputy 2 witnessed Deputy 1 murder my husband.

Declaration of (Timothy Warner)

I, (Timothy Warner) , hereby state and declare the following:

(1)   I am a competent adult who is over 18 years of age. I have personal knowledge of the following facts. With respect to those facts alleged on information and belief, I believe them to be true. If called to testify, I could and would testify consistently with the contents of this declaration.

(2)   I live in the City of (North Beach)   near the home of (Mrs. Sharp)   , which is located at (My Address)   . Prior to his death on March 27, 2015, (Mrs. Sharp's) late husband, (Patrick Sharp), also resided with (Mrs. Sharp) at (my address)

(3)   On March 27, 2015, at approximately 9:15 a.m., I let my dogs out for a walk and saw my neighbor,(Mrs. Sharp). She appeared very upset. She told me that her husband, (Patrick), was on the back patio of their house and that he had a gun and was threatening to kill himself.

(4)   I immediately ran over to the back patio of the   (Sharp)s' house. I looked over the fence and I saw (Patrick) holding what appeared to be a tactical shotgun under his chin. I yelled to him, "(Pat) don't do it!". I don't remember his precise response, but it was something like "get out of here".

(5)   I then ran down the alley by the garage and saw a Sheriff's car pulling up. The deputy asked me what was going on, and I told him that my neighbor had a gun and was suicidal. The deputy got on the radio and immediately called for back-up. Based upon my brief conversation with the deputy, my understanding was that the Sheriff's Department had been called because there was a 911 hang-up at (Mrs. Sharp) and (Patrick)'s house.

(6)   Within a few seconds of my conversation with the first deputy, I saw another deputy sheriff in police body armor holding an AR-15. This deputy moved very aggressively and I felt like something terrible was going to happen. His response seemed all wrong for the situation. I remember thinking to myself, "Oh no, are you kidding me? This is not going to end well."

(7)   I followed the deputy toward (Patrick) and (Mrs. Sharp)'s garage. (See the attached diagram.) The deputy took cover behind it. I was standing about 5 feet behind him. I could see the deputy with the AR-15, but I could not see (Pat) or what was happening on the grassy area by (Patrick) and (Mrs. Sharp)'s house.

(8)   I heard the deputy say words to the effect of, "Drop the gun, drop the gun". Very shortly after that – it seemed like a few seconds – the deputy fired the AR-15. It appeared to me that he fired two shots, paused for a second, and then fired two more. These events happened extremely quickly.

CHAPTER 15

The following are excerpts from Deputy 1's deposition, which took place two years after the incident. Please note that my attorney was much more thorough in his questioning than what is included here. I have changed the names of the persons and localities for privacy.

Like a juror in the courtroom, I encourage the reader to ultimately establish the truth for themselves.

● ● ●   I started at this part of the deposition because it was the first question of relevancy to compare with my version of the incident.

My Attorney:

```
20      Q    Why did you leave the patrol and go back to --
21   I understand you're working court fields now.  But why
22   did you leave patrol?
23      A    I wanted to get experience in other parts of
24   the department.
25      Q    So was it your choice to leave patrol, or were
1    you asked to leave patrol?
2       A    It was my choice.
```

● ● ●   Going from patrol to working in the court system is like an embarrassing demotion. He actually chose that for himself? A pretty dubious presumption.

```
5          Q    All right.  Do you have any military
6   experience?
7          A    Yes, sir.
12              I left the Marine Corps in 1993, and my job --
13  my MOS was as a HAWK Missile Systems Repair Technician.
14         Q    Were you ever deployed?
15         A    No, sir.
16         Q    So you never saw combat?
17         A    That is correct, sir.
```

• • •   This is important to remember.

```
6          Q    To your knowledge, was there an internal affair
7   investigation into this incident?
8          A    To my knowledge, I don't -- no, sir, I don't
9   know.
```

• • •   This is something he definitely *would* know!

```
14         Q    Were you disciplined in any way as a result of
15  this incident?
16         A    No, sir.
```

• • •   How could he have not been disciplined
for shooting his AR-15 in a residential
neighborhood?

```
24    Q    Have you ever been the subject of an internal

25  affair investigation in connection with your

1   Sheriff's Department employment involving allegations of

2   excessive force?

3       A    No, sir.

4       Q    To your knowledge, have you ever been the

5   subject of a complaint while working for  (Beach City)

6   Sheriff's Department alleging excessive force?

7       A    No, sir.
```

● ● ● My neighbor told me that the year before,
he had personally witnessed Deputy 1
harassing his roommate in front of their
house. Deputy 1 had stopped and asked
why the roommate was hanging out there.
The roommate told him that he lived
there. The roommate was from a Middle
Eastern country. Did Deputy 1 have
something against people from that part
of the world? (That's what it seemed like
to my neighbor). Deputy 1 was such an
asshole, that the roommate filed a formal
complaint against him.

Regarding my incident:

```
3       Q    Were you a one-man unit, or did you have a

4   partner that day?

5       A    I was a one-man unit.
```

2   Do you recall the specific comments of the

3   call, at least as it first came out?

4   A   If I recall, it came out just as a 9-1-1 hangup

5   from the residence. Dispatch attempted callback and got

6   no response, and then there were no further details.

7   Q   Okay. So at that point you responded to the

8   scene?

9   A   I began driving from the station. I left the

10 station and began driving to the location.

10   Q   All right. So en route you knew that (Deputy 2)

11 was responding --

12   A   Yes, sir.

13   Q   -- to this call as well and that he would be

14 the primary deputy?

15   A   Yes, sir.

16   Q   Okay. So what happened next en route to the

17 scene?

11   A   Deputy (2)   said that the man that had went to

12 the door at (My Address)   said the man that answered

13 the door had a shotgun, threatened to kill him,

14 threatened to shoot anybody that came up to the door.

2   Q   Is this the type of call that you would

3   typically request a supervisor respond to?

4   A   No, sir. We -- we generally want to assess the

81

5   scene first. We want to get there and -- and see what
6   we have.
7   Q   All right. Anything else happen en route to
8   the scene?
9   A   I pulled over real quick. I exited my vehicle
10   to go get my tactical vest that has medical supplies
11   affixed to the front of it.
12   And then I unlocked my department AR-15 rifle
13   from the -- from the brace that's affixed to the vehicle
14   that keeps it locked in the vehicle.

3   Q   So why did you stop and put your vest on and
4   unlock your AR-15 at that point?

9   I know that if -- based on my experience, that
10   somebody armed with a gun can leave their home. I
11   wanted to make sure that I had the appropriate supplies
12   with me or accessible to me quickly in case I was
13   confronted with somebody armed with a long gun that had
14   moved away from the location where they were last seen.
15   Q   All right. Did you have any idea as to the
16   type of gun that the individual at the residence was
17   allegedly armed with?
18   A   It was put out that the -- the man inside
19   (My Address)   had a shotgun.

25   Q   It was also a highly populated area; right?

```
2       A    It is a residential area, sir.

3       Q    There are a lot of different condominiums and

4    houses packed pretty densely in that area.  Would you

5    agree?

6       A    Yes, sir.
```

• • •   Yet, he still got his AR-15 ready to fire off
into the neighborhood.

```
13      Q    Prior to getting out of the car there on scene,

14   did you look up any additional information about this

15   call?

16      A    No, sir.


20      Q    Why not?

21      A    I wanted to get to (Deputy 2)  or within -- so I

22   could see (Deputy 2)   as soon as possible.  I felt

23   there was  an officer safety issue.


6            In your -- both your recorded interview and

7    your walk-through, though, you said that, when you

8    pulled up, you saw Deputy (2)    speaking with another

9    male.

10      A    Yes.  I could see him from -- from a distance.


14      Q    So I guess my question is:  Given the radio
```

15   issues that you generally have in that area and then

16   specifically en route to the scene hearing the robot and

17   not quite sure that you got all of the important

18   comments regarding the call, why not take a minute to

19   scroll through the comments on your MDC?

20   A   I didn't want to get shot. I know that area is

21   a grass area with a lot of open areas. I didn't want my

22   patrol car to become my casket. I wanted to get out as

23   soon as possible.

24   Q   All right.

25   Did you ask dispatch to provide you any

1   additional information about the call when you arrived?

2   A   No, sir.

3   Q   Why not?

4   A   I wanted to go talk to Deputy (2) .

● ● ●   But he didn't do that.

12   So, when you stepped out of your patrol car,

13   what equipment did you have with you?

14   A   I had my department-issued gun belt with all

15   the equipment that's on it.

16   Q   Okay. Which included what?

20   A set of handcuffs, OC spray, a Glock .22

21   department issued semiautomatic handgun, a taser, a

22 baton, and then two magazines with 15 rounds in each
23 magazine.

9   A   I had three firearms with me.

10   Q   Describe those.

11   A   I had my department issued AR-15, I had my

12 department issued Glock .22, and then I had my backup

13 Smith & Wesson 442 .38 Special revolver.

8   So, then, my question is: Prior to qualifying

9   in I think you said January of 2015, you had not been

10 issued an AR-15 with the Sheriff's Department prior to

11 that?

12   A   Correct, sir.

13   Q   So you qualified in January. But when were you

14 actually issued your AR-15 and allowed to start carrying

15 it with you on patrol?

16   A   You -- when you go through the class, that's

17 when they give you your -- or issue you your rifle.

18 That's the rifle that you go through the class with.

19 And, once you pass the class, that's the rifle that you

20 take with you on patrol.

21   Q   So you can basically take it home with you at

22 that point?

23   A   Yes, sir.

24   Q   Prior to this incident had you unlocked your

25 AR-15 at any call?

1   A   I don't -- I don't remember, sir.

● ● ●   I think that this is something he certainly *would* remember!

2   Q   So, as you sit here today, this call, as far as
3   you remember, was the first time you had ever unlocked
4   your AR-15 and actually brought it with you on a call?
5   A   Yes, sir.

9   At the time did you have a less lethal shotgun
10   with you?
11   A   I believe I had one in my trunk, sir.

5   Q   All right. And did you -- being interviewed by
6   Homicide detectives, were you truthful with them?
7   A   Yes, sir.
8   Q   Was there anything that you told them that was
9   not the truth?
10   A   No, sir.
11   Q   So, if you had told Homicide detectives that
12   you had both of these less than lethal weapon platforms
13   with you at the time, you have no reason to believe that
14   that was not the truth?
15   A   Correct, sir.
16   Q   So why did you take your AR-15 with you on this
17   call?

7 A I had made that decision once Deputy (2) had
8 initially put out over the air that the suspect was
9 armed with a shotgun.
10   When I had unlocked it on   (Street)   , I
11 knew that that -- that AR-15 was gonna come with me on
12 the call.

11   So at the time you arrived, what specifically
12 did you know about the call to which you were responding
13 and Mr. (Sharp) ?

5 A I knew nothing about Mr. (Sharp) . The only
6 thing that we had had earlier in the week was a briefing
7 about the general area.

19 Q And what was it that you heard had happened in
20 that area?
21 A We had been briefed that deputies had responded
22 to a domestic disturbance call -- I believe it was on a
23 Monday, Monday morning -- where the husband was throwing
24 items of clothing or -- items, clothing, and personal
25 belongings, outside of the residence.

1   And that when the deputies arrived there,
2 they -- they -- they were told there was a 1730, a
3 domestic dispute report, had been written, and that the

```
4   husband had -- had caught the wife having an

5   extramarital affair with another man inside the home,

6   and that's why the husband was upset and throwing stuff

7   out. And that's where it had been noted that there were

8   multiple guns on the property of an unknown type.


8        Q    During that briefing did they tell you that

9   PERT had responded during that previous incident?

10       A    No, sir. We weren't -- we weren't briefed on

11  that. The only thing we were briefed on was the -- the

12  415 and just the basic of the infidelity that occurred

13  in the home and why the husband was upset.

14       Q    Were you briefed that the husband was extremely

15  intoxicated when the deputies arrived?

16       A    No, sir.


3            I'm still responding to this as if there's

4   somebody -- it's a 9-1-1 hangup call. There's an armed

5   gunman inside the residence, and there could be

6   something -- somebody called 9-1-1, whether somebody in

7   the residence is being taken hostage or injured or

8   killed.

9            I'm not really concerned so much about the 415

10  family or any sort of infidelity. I'm -- at this point

11  I'm concerned who is in that residence right now. Who

12  might be in danger inside of that residence.
```

22   Q   Were you expecting a confrontation at the time
23 you stepped out of your patrol vehicle?
24   A   I was preparing for a confrontation. I
25 wasn't -- I wasn't -- I was hoping there wasn't gonna be
1   a confrontation.
2   But I would rather have had all the gear that I
3   needed with me just in case. I was hoping for a
4   peaceful resolution and hopefully that nobody was
5   injured.

2   Q   So you weren't aware that Mr. (Sharp)   was
3   despondent over a recent marital issue?
4   A   I had no idea that that residence,
5   Mr. (Sharp)   , was despondent over his marital issues.
6   Q   You had no idea whether Mr. (Sharp)   had been
7   drinking heavily?
8   A   I had no idea.
9   Q   You had no idea whether Mr. (Sharp)   was
10 suicidal?
11   A   I had no idea.
12   Q   So at the time you arrived there on scene you
13 didn't have any reason to believe that Mr.(Sharp)   had
14 threatened his wife in any way?

18   Q   So you, similarly, didn't have any reason to
19 believe that Mr. (Sharp)   was holding his wife hostage
20 when you arrived on scene?

21   A   I didn't know

● ● ●   He didn't know because he didn't stop to
         find out.

10   Q   What do you do when you get out of your patrol
11   vehicle?
12   A   I get out of my patrol vehicle. I take my
13   AR-15 with me. I pull the bolt back to the rear to put
14   a round in the chamber, and I take the weapon off safe
15   and then I start approaching Deputy (2) .
16   Q   Okay. So you actually charged your AR-15
17   before you even approached Deputy (2) ?
18   A   Yes, sir.
19   Q   Okay. Are you walking or are you running at
20   this point?
21   A   I'm just walking.

22   Q   Okay. What do you do next?
23   A   I walk over to Deputy (2) , and I kind of look
24   at -- I'm -- I don't know having -- like I said, I don't
25   have any further updates. I don't know who he's talking
 1   to.

9   So I'm kind of walking tentatively just to make

10   sure that this isn't our suspect. I don't see any

11   shotgun in his hand. I don't see any weapons visible.

12   So, while I'm alert and scanning the area to

13   make sure we're not gonna get ambushed, I'm also looking

14   to see what Deputy   (2) 's demeanor is talking to this

15   gentleman as I'm approaching him.

16   Q   Do you ever ask Deputy   (2)   who the guy is

17   that he's talking to?

18   A   I walk over to Deputy   (2)   and I -- I asked

19   him -- gosh, I can't even recall what I asked.

> **• • •** He couldn't remember because he didn't
> stop to communicate. He was hell-bent on
> his own agenda.

20   I remember asking where the apartment was in

21   specific to where he was. And I could see Deputy

22   (2) , it looked like he was writing -- it looked like

23   he had his deputy's notebook and some information in his

24   hand. I don't recall ever asking him who that person

25   was.

1   Q   So, as you're approaching the position, Deputy

2   (2)   and this individual, how do you have your rifle?

3   A   As I'm approaching I have it down at the -- you

4   know, kind of down at the low ready. I'm not aiming at

5   anybody or -- I'm scanning the areas around us just to

91

6   make sure that we're not getting approached either front

7   or back.

8   Q   Do you remember anything else that you said to

9   Deputy (2) ?

10   A   I believe I told him -- or I asked him where

11 the apartment was. And, since he didn't give me the --

12 the Code 4 sign or that everything is good to go, I told

13 him I was gonna go try and get eyes on the apartment

14 just so that we could set up, you know, where we could

15 establish other units. Just kind of set up a perimeter

16 position.

23   Q   What specifically did Deputy (2)   say to you,

24 if anything?

25   A   I believe he said it's -- he kind of pointed

1   down in the north direction and said, "It's just

2   around" -- like north and around the corner.

17   And you're positive that you told Deputy (2)

18 you were going to go put eyes on the subject?

19   A   I believe I said that, sir. I believe I said I

20 was gonna go -- not on the suspect. I was gonna go get

21 eyes on the apartment because I wanted to -- we

22 generally try to have -- get a position of cover, get a

23 position of containment so if somebody is inside their

24 home we don't -- with an -- armed with a weapon, we

25 don't want them walking out into a public location.

5   Well, I'll represent to you that Deputy (2)
6   testified under oath yesterday that the only thing you
7   said to him was, basically, "Where is the house?"
8   A   Okay.
9   Q   Nothing beyond that.

1   I again will represent to you that Deputy (2)
2   testified that you asked him where the location was as
3   you walked past. You never actually stopped.
4   A   Yes, sir. I never stopped.
5   Q   Okay.

1   Q   So you at no point spoke with Mr. (Warner)   , the
2   individual that Deputy (2)   was speaking to?
3   A   No, sir.
4   Q   As you walked past, did Mr. (Warner) say anything
5   to you or say anything to Deputy (2)   that you
6   overheard?
7   A   Not that I recall, sir.
8   Q   So can you describe your approach through these
9   garages?

18   So my weapon is trained forward, and I'm
19 walking forward with a purpose. I want to get out -- we
20 call that the fatal funnel, and I want to try and get
21 out of there as soon as possible.

22   Q   So you would agree that being inside that row

23 of garages like that is not a tactically sound position

24 to be in?

25   A   It's not a comfortable. Tactically it is in

1   relation to where the apartment is, because it provides

2   me cover and concealment.

9   Q   So what was the critical need for you to leave

10 your partner there on scene and charge ahead and make

11 contact with this residence by yourself?

12   A   I wasn't -- I wasn't gonna make contact with

13 anything. I was gonna look and survey the area, see if

14 I could locate the residence.

15   Q   Okay.

16   Well, you've already described this as a fatal

17 funnel where an individual could sneak up behind you if

18 he wanted to; right?

19   A   Yes, sir.

20   Q   Don't you think it would have been safer for

21 yourself to have waited for Deputy (2)   to make that

22 approach with you and cover your rear?

23   A   No, sir. Sometimes you have to -- you have to

24 make a decision. You have to make a decision that --

25 what you're gonna do.

21   Q   You don't think it would have been safer for

22 Deputy (2)   to have waited for him to finish with the

23 witness and approach together?

24   A   No, sir. Because, if he was here, he already
25   had this area covered.

12   Q   Did you tell Deputy (2) to cover that area?
13   A   No, sir.
14   Q   Did Deputy (2) tell you that he was covering
15   that area?
16   A   No, sir.
17   Q   Did Deputy (2) have his gun drawn while he
18   was talking to this witness?
19   A   That I don't recall, sir. I don't think so,
20   but I don't recall.
21   Q   You said he had his notebook out, and he was
22   writing in it; right?
23   A   Yes, sir.
24   Q   So, based on that, it seems fair to assume that
25   he did not also have his firearm out.

3   I will represent to you that Deputy (2)
4   testified under oath that when he saw you advance to
5   that corner -- he was not expecting you to advance to
6   the corner but, when he saw you there, he quickly put
7   his notebook away, drew his gun and ran to catch up with
8   you to cover you.

• • •   This explains how I saw two deputies
aiming their guns at Patrick.

95

9   So would you agree that if he's running to
10   catch up with you to cover you, he's probably not
11   advancing tactically through that fatal funnel that you
12   described?
13   A   I don't know, sir. I don't know which
14   direction his -- his weapon was pointed.
15   Q   So you -- in looking back at this you do not
16   think that it put -- your charging ahead and contacting
17   the residence by yourself put Deputy (2)   in a
18   less-than-safe position?
19   A   No, sir.

19   Q   Okay. What did you do when you reached the
20   corner?
21   A   When I reached the corner, I started doing what
22   we call cutting the pie.
23   Q   Describe that.
24   A   That's where you -- or that's where you start
25   looking -- I looked to the right and surveyed over here
1   grass.
2   Q   All right.
3   A   I didn't know who he was. I saw a man.
4   Q   How soon after you arrived there at the corner
5   was it before you spotted this man?
6   A   A few seconds. A few -- maybe not even a few
7   seconds. I'm cutting the pie quickly.

11   Did you point your rifle at this individual on

```
12    the grass as soon as you saw him?

13         A    I saw that he had a shotgun in his hand so,

14    yes, I was -- I had my weapon aimed at him.

15         Q    All right.

16              So please describe this individual when you

17    first saw him.

18         A    When I saw -- when I came to that point in my

19    vision, I saw a guy -- I saw a man sitting in the grass.

20    Had a shotgun in his -- in his hands.
```

• • •   This can't be what he saw, because
          Patrick was never sitting in the grass.

```
25              He kind of -- he was kind of sweaty.  And it

1     looked like there was like a bottle -- there was like a

2     large bottle with like a red label on it that I would

3     recognize as either a generic form of vodka or Popov.

4     It had the look of a Popov label.
```

```
8               Anything else you remember about this

9     individual when you first saw him?

10         A    He just had the -- the shotgun was in his

11    hand, and it was -- either it looked like it was next to

12    his -- the left side of his face or it was under his

13    chin.  I couldn't really tell at that distance exactly

14    where it was.  But the barrel was pointing upwards.
```

16   Q   So, using Exhibit 10, I will represent to you

17 that this is Mr. (Sharp)   under this yellow fire

18 blanket. This is where he came -- he ultimately ended

19 up after Deputy (5)   and Sergeant (6)   rolled him

20 over to do CPR on him. Based on testimony from the

21 previous witnesses, he hadn't been moved after that.

18   Q   Okay. So he was facing directly towards you?

19   A   No. He was -- if this is the row of garages,

20 if I'm -- if I'm Mr. (Sharp)   , if this is the row of

21 garages or the walkway where I'm standing and this is

22 the sidewalk where the -- that kind of goes in front of

23 the condos, he would have been seated looking that way

24 towards the sidewalk.

```
4        Q    Okay.  The way I heard your testimony I thought
5    he was facing one way but looking another way.
6        A    No, no.  I'm sorry.  His body was looking --
7    like he's waiting for somebody to come down the
8    sidewalk.  He's looking down the sidewalk.
```

> ● ● ●   Patrick was never looking down the
> sidewalk. He was standing motionless
> facing both deputies with their guns aimed
> at him.

```
10            So you said that you believed he had the
11   shotgun under his chin?
12       A    He had it in a way that I couldn't -- I
13   couldn't tell.  It was -- it was either next to his
14   face, or it was under his chin, but I couldn't --
15   spatially I couldn't -- I couldn't make out -- I didn't
16   have enough time to make out the difference.
```

> ● ● ●   That's because he wasted no time in
> shooting him.

```
18            Well, in your recorded interview, you said you
19   saw Mr. (Sharp)  sitting on the grass with the shotgun
20   under his chin.  You also saw the 1.75 liter of alcohol
21   next to his feet.
```

6   Q   How was it resting? Did it appear that he had

7   his chin resting on the barrel?

8   A   No. That's -- if I had seen that, then I would

9   have been able to see the indent, or I would have seen

10   that it was under his chin if I had seen it resting.

11   Q   But you do recall that in your interview you

12   described it as the gun being under his chin.

13   A   Right. I described it -- I should have been

14   more careful that it appeared that it may have been

15   under his chin is.

16   Q   Okay. Which hand was he holding it with?

17   A   He had -- if I believe, he had the -- I think

18   he had both hands.

19   Q   And, you know, this might be a good opportunity

20   to use our replica gun to begin with.

24   Q   Deputy, I will represent to you this is

25   incapable of firing. There's nothing that it can

1   shoot.

2   Would you mind using that to demonstrate how

3   you recall seeing Mr. (Sharp)   holding the shotgun when

4   you first saw him on the grass?

5   A   Okay. He had it in his -- he had the fore-end

6   in his -- the fore-end being the part that -- in a pump

7   action shotgun, you actually pump. He had the fore-end

8   under -- on -- with -- he's holding it with his left

9   hand, and I don't think I was able to see his right

10   hand. I don't know if his right hand was resting or if

11   he just had it close by. I don't recall where his

12   right hand was in relationship to the shotgun at that

13   time.

       • • •   Where both of his hands are seems to be pretty important knowing that it takes two hands to fire a shotgun.

14   Q   Okay. And it was his right side that was

15   facing you; correct?

16   A   No. It would have been his left side that was

17   facing me. If I'm over here --

18   Q   Okay. I'm sorry. You're right. I was

19   thinking -- I was thinking left, but I said right.

20   So, because he's facing this way, he's holding

21   it on the side that is facing you?

22   A   The shotgun is on my side.

23   Q   Okay. All right.

24   And he was holding it like that, and that led

25   you to believe that it might have been under his chin?

1   A   Well, no. I'm not -- I'm not -- he had it --

2   he had it resting on his -- on his knee. He had it

3   lower, and he was kind of leaning -- almost leaning

4   back, kind of like sitting backwards. Like back. I

5   don't know if he had sat up, but it seemed like he was

6   leaning back a little bit.

```
 7      Q    I see.  And, because of the length of the

 8   shotgun, if he had wanted to put it under his chin, he

 9   probably would have had to have leaned back to get it

10   under there?

11      A    He could have.  Or he could have just been

12   leaning back in the grass.


14      A    But at this -- something at this distance from

15   looking about 25, 30 yards away quickly, I could only

16   see that -- where it was in relationship that it's --

17   the barrel might be parallel with his chin but not

18   necessarily underneath it.


11      Q    How were his legs?

12      A    His legs were out in front of him.  He was kind

13   of -- I try -- I try and think about how he was -- you

14   know, I say lying or leaning.

15           He was kind of in a position where his legs

16   were bent, and he was just kind of leaning back, but he

17   wasn't fully lying but he wasn't fully sitting up

18   either.  He was kind of in a -- in a back position.


24      Q    All right.  Were his legs crossed?

25      A    I don't believe so.  I don't remember seeing

 1   his legs crossed.

 2      Q    Well, if he was leaning back as far as you say,
```

3   did you see him -- did you see his feet under anything

4   to get leverage?

5   You know like say, for instance, when you want

6   to do situps somewhere, you kind of leverage your feet

7   under something?

8   A   I didn't see his feet under anything.

9   Q   So would that lead you to believe that his legs

10   were crossed, then? If he were leaning like that, how

11   else would you keep your balance from tipping over?

12   A   I don't know. Again, I don't know if I caught

13   him in mid -- if he had fallen over, and he was trying

14   to sit back up. I don't know why he ended up in the

15   position I saw him. I can't --

16   Q   When you saw him, what did he do? Did he stay

17   suspended like that?

18   A   When I saw him, I keyed up my radio and, as

19   soon as he heard my voice, he jumped up. He was in the

20   position of sitting up.

5   Q   He stood up at that point?

6   A   He stood up.

7   Q   All right. So you didn't say anything to him

8   prior to him standing up?

9   A   I might have told him to stay where he was. I

10   don't really recall.

11   Q   All right. Does he say anything to you before

12   standing up?

13   A   No, sir. He starts -- he starts yelling -- I

14   mean, he may have said something. I don't recall. It

15   was pretty much immediate me giving him commands to put

16   the gun down and him starting to yell and starting to

17   yell, "Shoot me" with us both yelling over the top of

18   each other.

19   Q   Okay. So did you -- you said you pointed your

20   rifle at him as soon as you saw him?

21   A   Yes, sir. As soon as -- because I was already

22   cutting the pie. So, as soon as I came around and saw

23   him, he was already in my -- he was already in my

24   sights.

25   Q   So did you keep your rifle pointed -- trained

1   on Mr. (Sharp)   while you put out over the radio --

2   A   Yes, sir. I had my -- I had my microphone on

3   my left shoulder. So I was able to brace it into my --

4   the buttstock into my right arm and key up real quick.

5   Q   All right.

6   So, as you sit here today, do you remember

7   saying anything to Mr. (Sharp)   before you put out over

8   the radio that you see the suspect in the grass?

9   A   No, sir.

11   A   When Mr. (Sharp)   stood up, he -- his body

12   moved to my right. He became -- he faced me directly,

13   and he moved this way (indicating). So it would be his

14   left, my right. At that point he's fully looking --

15   he's looking straight on at me.

16   Q   Okay. At what point do you first speak to
17 Mr. (Sharp) ?
18   A   When I'm giving him commands to stay where he
19 is and then start dropping the weapon. The commands
20 are immediate. I'm not -- when I see him with a
21 shotgun, it's not conversation time. It's me giving
22 commands.
23   Q   So do you -- you're not sure if you gave him
24 any commands while he was sitting on the ground?
25   A   He was -- as soon as I keyed up, he was
1   starting to stand. And I told him -- I think I told
2   him, "Stay where you're at" or "Stay on the ground." I
3   can't remember.
4   Q   So about how far away was Mr. (Sharp)   from you
5   when you first saw him?
6   A   Maybe 25 yards.

7   Q   And was the gun between his legs?

8   A   Not anymore. When he stood up with it, it was

9   in his left hand.

10   Q   But when he was on the ground, the gun was

11   between his legs?

12   A   That I don't know. I can't remember if it was

13   next to him. I just saw the gun. I wasn't -- at that

14   point then -- I'm kind of weapon fixated at this point.

15   Q   All right.

16   Well, in your recorded interview you said when

17   you first saw Mr. (Sharp)   on the ground, his knees were

18   up and the gun was between them.

19   A   It could have been. He's wearing black shorts,

20   and the gun is black. And at this point I'm weapon

21   fixated. So I could believe that at that time.

22   But looking back on it, I don't know if the gun

23   was between his legs or if the gun was next to him --

24   next to him.

1   Well, do you have any reason to believe what

2   you told Homicide detectives a couple of hours after

3   this happened was not true?

4   A   No. I -- I have no reason to believe that.

5   Q   But you do remember Mr. (Sharp)   holding the

6   gun by the slide with his left hand --

7   A   Yes, sir.

8   Q   -- leaning back and, whether it was to the side

9   of his left leg or between his legs, at this point you

10   don't remember?

11   A   I can't remember.

         • • •   A liar has the burden of remembering
                  their earlier lies to the word, lest they get
                  caught in their own trap.

2   Q   Was he saying anything or making any noises

3   when you first saw him?

4   A   I don't remember hearing him saying anything.

6   So in your recorded interview you said that you

7   told Mr. (Sharp)   to put the gun on the ground two to

8   three times, and Mr. (Sharp)   looked at you and said

9   something intelligible -- unintelligible and then told

10   you to shoot him. Mr. (Sharp)   then stood up and said,

11   "Shoot me."

12   A   Everything was happening so fast. I don't know

13   if -- he was yelling things at -- right after I keyed

14   up, he turned to look at me, and it was -- he was

15   standing up.

16   So at that -- everything -- he was yelling at

17   the time that he saw me. It was as soon as I -- as soon

18   as he heard my voice and looked over at me, he was

19   moving and yelling, and I was giving commands.

● ● ●   Patrick was never moving or yelling.

3   Q   Okay. So you think all of that happened
4   basically simultaneous?
5   A   Pretty simultaneously, yes.

7   So, in reviewing what you had said previously,
8   does that refresh your recollection as to whether or not
9   you gave Mr. (Sharp)   any commands while he was still
10   seated on the ground?
11   A   My initial command would have been to -- if I
12   recall, was just, "Stay where you're at." It would have
13   been something along those lines.

17   But upon seeing me and that initial command, he
18   was already moving. So while I'm talking, he's moving.
19   While I'm giving commands, he's moving to the -- I mean,
20   every -- he's moving to face me.

24   Q   So you saw the vodka bottle there, or what you
25   believed to be a vodka bottle.

1   A   Yes, sir.
2   Q   Did he appear intoxicated?
3   A   I couldn't tell, sir.
4   Q   Well, the fact that he's got that size of a

5 bottle of alcohol next to him and, you know, it wasn't
  6 even 10:00 yet, an officer with your experience, did
  7 that lead you to believe this guy has probably been
  8 drinking this morning?

  9   A   I wouldn't have been able to make that
 10 determination. It could have been a vodka bottle that
 11 was just left by somebody, some transient or something
 12 along those lines. I wouldn't have known that he was in
 13 possession of that. That just was there in the vicinity
 14 of where he was.

 15   Q   Did the possibility that he was highly
 16 intoxicated factor into your calculation at any point
 17 during this incident?

 18   A   No, sir.

 19   Q   So you were operating under the assumption that
 20 Mr. (Sharp)   was not intoxicated, that he could fully
 21 hear you and fully understand and fully comprehend the
 22 commands you were giving him?

 23   A   I was hoping that Mr. (Sharp)   would
 24 understand and -- and comprehend the instructions. I
 25 wasn't gonna assume that he did. I was hoping that he
  1 would.

  2   Q   So you didn't change your tactics at all based
  3 on the potentiality that he could be highly intoxicated
  4 at this point?

  5   A   No, sir.

  6   Q   So how does Mr. (Sharp)   get on his feet?

  7   A   He stands. I'm -- I'm watching -- I'm keeping

8   my eyes on that muzzle of that weapon at this time.   I'm

9   not really focusing on what Mr.   (Sharp)'s feet are

10   doing or what his -- you know, where he's looking.   I'm

11   watching that -- the muzzle of that weapon to see where

12   it's gonna go.

13   Q   All right.

14   So does he set the gun down, stand up, then

15   reach over and pick it up?

16   A   No, sir.   He -- he stands up with the gun

17   straight up in his hand.

18   Q   Okay.

19   Did you at any point learn that there was a

20   toxicology panel performed after Mr.   (Sharp)'s death

21   which showed he was -- had a BAC of .28 at the time of

22   the incident?

23   A   I learned about that later, sir.

24   Q   And do you have any experience with DUI

25   enforcement or with dealing with intoxicated

1   individuals?

2   A   I've taken a DUI class, and I've seen people

3   that have been drunk in public.

4   Q   So, then, you are aware that a .28 percent BAC

5   is pretty high?

6   A   It can be.   It can also be baseline for

7   somebody that's an alcoholic.

8   Q   Sure.   You're still going to have pretty severe

9   motor impairment at .28, even if you're a chronic

10   alcohol drinker.

11   A   Not necessarily. A .28 with a chronic

12 alcoholic could make the baseline where they're not

13 experiencing symptoms of withdrawal so they could act as

14 if somebody is normal.

15   That's what the baseline means where they

16 function normally, but they have to have an elevated

17 blood alcohol content level to function normally.

18   Q   So your understanding is that somebody at .28,

19 even if a chronic alcohol user, there's going to be

20 little to no motor impairment?

21   A   There may be some motor impairment but not in a

22 way that wouldn't be -- may not be visible without

23 further evaluation.

24   Upon initial -- initial sight you might not see

25 some of those gross -- or fine, gross or fine motor

1 skills functions deteriorate. But after a lengthy

2 evaluation talking to that person, you might see that.

3   Q   I wish I would have had you as a deputy in some

4 of my DUI trials as a young attorney.

8   Q   Okay. So you didn't have any reason to believe

9 at this point that Mr. (Sharp)   was a chronic alcohol

10 drinker; right?

11   A   No.

12   Q   So you had no idea?

13   A   I had no idea, sir.

14   Q   So you would agree, though, that that is pretty

15 intoxicated?

111

16   A   For a normal person, that is. That is --
17 that's a high blood alcohol content.

18   Q   That's somebody who has been drinking very,
19 very hard in the preceding hours.

20   A   Yes, sir.

21   Q   So, when he stood up, you didn't see him
22 stumble, you didn't see him labor to get onto his feet
23 at all?

24   A   No, sir. He was actually pretty -- he was
25 actually pretty surefooted. He stood up very quickly
1 and was quick to face me.

2   Q   Do you see Ms. (Sharp)   at this point?

3   A   I never saw Ms. (Sharp)   until later on.

4   Q   You didn't see her prior to firing your first
5 shots?

6   A   No, sir.

**• • •   Yes he did. He was yelling at me to
get back so that he could proceed
with his plan to shoot Patrick.**

8   So what happens with the shotgun as
9 Mr. (Sharp)   stands up?

10   A   He stands up, and he -- he extends both of his
11 arms out like he's in a cross with his arms parallel to
12 the ground.

13   And he has the shotgun in his left hand, and

14 he's still holding it by the fore-end with the muzzle
15 pointed straight up.

17   You said in your recorded interview that, based
18 on what you saw, at this point you believed Mr. (Sharp)
19 had made the decision to take his own life.
20   A   I believe that he was -- with him yelling,
21 "Shoot me" and, again, we were -- I was giving commands,
22 and what I did hear him say a couple times was, "Shoot
23 me."
24   He was yelling other things in between as I was
25 yelling over the top of him. I believe that he may have
1 been trying to do suicide by cop.
2   Q   When you first saw him with the shotgun, what
3 appeared to you at least initially to be under his chin,
4 did you think this is an individual that's about to take
5 his own life?
6   A   It had the potential.
7   Q   So at that point you had a very strong
8 indication that this individual was suicidal?
9   A   When he stood up with the shotgun and started
10 yelling, "Shoot me," yes.

2   Q   So you think within five seconds of arriving at
3 that corner he had already stood up?
4   A   Probably less than that.
5   Q   Less than five seconds?
6   A   Probably -- probably maybe less than that.

13   Q   So when he was sitting there with what appeared

14   to be the shotgun under his chin, I mean, that

15   technically is not illegal; right?

16   A   Well, he's brandishing a firearm in public.

17   It's a public -- it's a place that's open to the public.

18   So what we have right there is -- could be a 417 PC,

19   brandishing a firearm.

20   Q   Is he brandishing it, though?

21   A   Well, he's holding it. And we've had a -- we

22   have a -- a report from a third party saying that they

23   had a shotgun -- they were threatened with life with a

24   man with a shotgun.

25   So at this point he's -- he's probably --

1   probably -- probable -- my suspect.

3   But you -- at least when I initially asked you,

4   you didn't believe you had probable cause to arrest him

5   for anything when you saw him.

6   A   I wasn't -- I hadn't even begun my

7   investigation. I develop probable cause as I conduct an

8   investigation.

9   Q   All right.

10   So what specifically had -- instructions had

11   you given to Mr. (Sharp)   up to this point?

12   A   I believe I told him to -- when I first saw him

13   to stay where he was or to remain where he was.

14   And then several times to put the weapon on the

15 ground and get on the ground. I don't know how many
16 times I said it. I know I said it really loud. I was
17 pretty much yelling it.

● ● ●   Deputy 1 yelled at me to get back. Then he
         yelled "Drop your weapon!" twice. That
         was it.

18   And -- but I couldn't tell you exactly what the
19 verbiage was. Just in that moment, "Get on the ground."
20 "Drop the weapon." "Put the gun down." He's yelling,
21 and I'm yelling.
22   Q   All right.
23   If you didn't have reasonable suspicion to
24 detain him or probable cause to arrest him, is that a
25 lawful command?
1   A   He's holding a firearm. I'm developing -- I
2   need to make the scene safe. For officer safety
3   purposes I need to make sure that the scene is safe
4   while I conduct an investigation.
5   And at the time I have a suspect or subject in
6   the grass between me and that condo with a weapon. The
7   scene isn't safe. So the officer safety comes into play
8   here before I can even start an investigation.

14   Q   What is the standard of proof that has to be
15 met before you can detain a suspect?

16   A   You have to have reasonable suspicion that a

17   crime is about to be -- has been committed or will be

18   committed.

• • •   *So why was I detained?*

19   Q   Okay.

20   So is there an exception to that, saying you

21   can detain somebody even if you don't have reasonable

22   suspicion if it's for officer safety?

1   Right now I have to make sure the scene is

2   safe. I'm not going to detain him with a shotgun in his

3   hands. He needs to comply with me 100 percent.

4   Q   Even if you don't have reasonable suspicion to

5   detain him?

6   A   I have 835 PC.

7   Q   Which is an exception to the Fourth Amendment?

8   A   No. It's not an exception to the Fourth

9   Amendment. It's that if I am about to make a detention

10   or arrest, I don't have to retreat. He has to follow my

11   commands.

12   And I'm not under any sort of punishable --

13   can't be punished by law for doing that. I believe

14   that's 835 PC.

15   Q   Okay. Well, I'm not asking you about the

16   California Penal Code. I'm asking you about the Fourth

17   Amendment to the U.S. Constitution.

18   A   Okay.

19   Q   You don't -- you just testified you did not

20   think that you had reasonable suspicion to detain

21   Mr. (Sharp)   at this point, but you're giving him

22   commands.

23   A   He's -- he is in an area open to the public

24   with a shotgun. He is not -- he's not in his home.

25   He's not within his curtilage. He's brandishing a

1   weapon.

2   Q   Well, you don't know where his home is at this

3   point.

4   A   I don't know -- I don't even know who this

5   person is.

6   Q   Okay. So -- which is even more of an argument

7   as to why he's not violating any laws at this point.

8   A   He's carrying an open -- he's carrying a weapon

9   in public. That's a violation of the California Penal

10   Code.

11   Q   Okay. 417?

12   A   That's brandishing a weapon. Yes.

13   Q   What are the elements of brandishing?

14   A   Brandishing is having a weapon in a public area

15   that's open to the public.

16   Q   Any weapon?

17   A   Any weapon that can cause physical harm or

18   death to somebody.

117

12   Q   So he -- how many times did he yell at you to
13   shoot him?
14   A   If I had to guess, three or four.

● ● ●   Patrick said it once, in a regular sounding
           voice. And that's the last thing he said
           audibly before he was gunned down.

23   Q   Did his speech sound slurred?
24   A   He just sounded loud and angry.

3   Q   And you didn't detect any slur in his speech?
4   A   No, sir.

13   Q   At what point did you first see Ms. (Sharp)   ?
14   A   After I had fired the second -- the fourth
15   round, and Mr. (Sharp)   landed on his -- face down on
16   his stomach.
17   And Mrs. (Sharp)   -- or a female went running
18   towards the body from the sidewalk. From the -- from
19   that area. From that other side of the garage. I'm not
20   exactly sure where she came from.
21   Q   All right.
22   In your walk-through, which was also audio
23   recorded, you there again said Mr. (Sharp)   said, "Shoot
24   me. Shoot me," then stood up.
25   A   Everything was happening simultaneously.

2   So would you mind using our toy shotgun again?

3   And just demonstrating -- after Mr. (Sharp)   stands up,

4   how does he come to face you, and what is the shotgun

5   doing at that point?

6   A   Okay. Mr. (Sharp)   faces me and then he

7   does -- he's doing this (indicating). He's got the gun

8   out in his left hand holding it by the fore-end, and his

9   right hand is out away from his body. He's almost kind

10   of in a cross pose.

11   Q   Does he have the vodka bottle in his right

12   hand?

13   A   No, sir. His right hand is open.

14   Q   And do you know where the vodka bottle is at

15   this point?

16   A   I'm not even looking for the vodka bottle at

17   this point.

19   So how long is Mr. (Sharp)   in the position

20   that you're demonstrating right now?

21   A   Seconds.

25   Q   Okay. So, while he's like that, is he telling

1   you to shoot him?

2   A   Yes, sir.

3   Q   All right. And are you giving him commands

4   while he's like that?

5   A   Yes, sir.

6   Q   What are you saying?

7   A   I'm saying, "Put the gun down. Get on the

8 ground. Put the gun down. Drop the weapon." Something

9 along those lines.

14   He starts swinging the -- he takes a -- he took

15 a step forward, and the barrel started swinging towards

16 me and his right hand starts going towards the pistol

17 grip of the shotgun.

18   Q   Okay. Does it ever actually get into that

19 position?

20   A   No. I -- it starts in this motion. And by

21 about here (indicating) is when I start firing. I fired

22 the initial three shots.

Patrick was standing this way the entire time before he was shot.

24   How long does it take Mr. (Sharp)   to get from

25   the perpendicular position that you're in to where

1   you -- as far as you said he got before you fired?

2   A   Milliseconds.

3   Q   So, while he was holding the gun perpendicular,

4   the barrel was pointing straight up; right?

5   A   Yes, sir.

6   Q   It was not pointing in your direction?

7   A   Yes, sir.

8   Q   Okay.

9   So, when Mr. (Sharp)   made the motion you just

10   described where he brought his arms down from the

11   perpendicular position, he still had his hand on the

12   fore-end of the shotgun?

13   A   Yes, sir.

14   Q   The pump?

15   A   Yes, sir. In that vicinity.

16   Q   And that was his left hand?

17   A   Yes, sir.

18   Q   So you would agree that holding the shotgun

19   with the left hand by the fore-end, you cannot fire the

20   shotgun when it's being held like that?

21   A   I would agree with that, sir.

22   Q   Okay. So you eventually fire your AR-15?

23   A   Yes, sir.

24   Q   While Mr. (Sharp)   is in that position where

25   his arms are out perpendicular, are you still in the

1   same position as when you first saw Mr. (Sharp) ?

2   A   I have moved with -- he's moved to his left, my

```
 3   right. And I'm still standing in the position where I'm
 4   at. We're facing each other now.


11        Q    So you think the first three shots it was
12   that -- it was a sequence like that, boom, boom, boom?
13        A    Probably faster.
14        Q    Faster than that?
15        A    Yeah.  Boom, boom, boom.
16        Q    Now, what was your background at the time you
17   fired those first three rounds?
18        A    I know there was a -- there was a -- it looked
19   like another -- either a house or another condo complex
20   over here (indicating).


12        A    Yes, sir.  I remember it being the -- there was
13   some buildings in -- in my background.
14        Q    Okay.
15             And did you see any other people out, any
16   civilians or pedestrians out in that area?
17        A    No, sir.  When I was watching Mr. (Sharp)    --
18   like I said, things were happening simultaneously.
19             We're taught in the academy to look at -- look
20   at our backdrop, to watch the suspect.  And, with the
21   backdrop as it is, I was able to scan and see that I
22   didn't see anybody moving in the background, and I was
23   also watching Mr.   (Sharp)'s right hand.
```

122

6   And at the time I wasn't able to see behind

7   Mr. (Sharp)   's back. Had to make sure that while I was

8   paying attention to his left hand holding the shotgun,

9   he wouldn't reach into a pocket or reach behind his

10   waistband, behind his back, and remove a firearm and use

11   it on me then.

12   So I was paying attention to a lot of different

13   things. Backdrop, Mr.   (Sharp) 's right hand, and the

14   shotgun as all this -- and giving commands as all this

15   is happening. There was a lot of things going on.

23   Q   Okay. You're giving commands to Mr. (Sharp)   .

24   A   Yes, sir.

25   Q   You're paying attention to the barrel of the

1   shotgun.

2   A   Yes, sir.

3   Q   You're also paying attention to his right

4   hand.

5   A   Yes, sir.

6   Q   And you're also scanning the background to make

7   sure you've got a clear field of fire.

8   A   Yes, sir.

9   Q   And this all happens within seconds?

10   A   Yes, sir.

11   Q   Were you worried at all about those houses

12   behind Mr. (Sharp)   when you fired?

13   A   Yes, sir.

14   Q   Why were you worried about that?

15   A   I knew at the proximity where I was standing

16   and where Mr. (Sharp)   was standing that firing rounds

17   from that AR-15, that those rounds were gonna go quickly

18   if I hit Mr. (Sharp)   . Or if I did not hit him, they

19   were still gonna go quickly. And they had the potential

20   to go into the homes or the walls behind me. Or the

21   walls, the ground and skip off.

22   Q   How many feet per second do 223 rounds travel?

23   A   I don't really know. I can't recall, sir.

24   Q   Do you know how far they'll travel?

25   A   I know in the Marine Corps we could use -- with

1   556, which is a little bit less, we could -- we could

2   strike bullseyes from about 500 yards.

5   Q   About how far behind Mr. (Sharp)   would you say

6   those additional residences were?

7   A   Maybe 40 yards. 30, 40 yards maybe.

23   Q   So, when you fire shot one, what specifically

24   is Mr. (Sharp)   doing? Has he just started to lower the

25   gun from the parallel position?

1   A   No, sir. He's already -- he's already

2   committed to going into a shooting stance.

3   His -- the barrel has -- has closed the

4   distance to the point where, if I hadn't shot that first

5   round, he probably could have gotten everything together

6   and shot one round towards me.

24   Q   How fast does he -- how fast does Mr. (Sharp)

25   do it?

1   A   Very quickly.

13   Q   Okay. So the barrel never actually pointed in

14   your direction?

15   A   It was moving in my direction, but I wasn't

16   allow -- going to have a barrel -- I wasn't gonna let a

17   barrel come square into my -- I wasn't gonna face my

18   death with a -- with a shotgun barrel.

19   Q   All right.

20   So what does Mr. (Sharp)   do after shot --

21   after you fire shot one?

22   A   He's still -- I fire three shots. After the

23   third shot, he falls. So he's still standing after my

24   first shot. He's still standing after my second shot.

25   It's after the third shot he falls straight

1   backward. So up until the third shot, he's still

2   standing.

3   Q   Okay.

4   But does the gun move any more after you fire

5   the first shot?

6   A   I don't believe so. At this point I'm --

7   I'm -- my -- I'm looking through my sights. I'm more

8   focused on my sight picture than --

10   So that motion that you were making, you

11 demonstrated where he was when you fired the first shot.

12 After that first shot that motion stops?

13   A   I believe so. I wasn't really paying attention

14 to the motion anymore. I was more focused on what I was

15 doing with the rifle.

6   Q   So, after you fired shot two, did -- what did

7   Mr. (Sharp)   do?

8   A   He was still standing.

9   Q   Still standing. And he's -- his arms were

10 still in the same position as when you fired shot one?

11   A   I believe so, sir.

12   Q   Could you tell if shot one hit him?

13   A   I couldn't tell.

14   Q   Could you tell if shot two hit him?

15   A   No, sir.

16   Q   All right. So your positioning didn't change

17 for shot three either?

18   A   Unless -- unless it just moved away from the

19 barrel. But standing-wise, I remember standing where I

20 was standing.

21   Q   Okay. And Mr. (Sharp)   's position didn't

22 move --

23   A   He didn't move left or right. He stayed

24 | stationary where he was.

25 | Q   And were his arms in the same position as they

1 | were for shot one right before you fired shot three?

2 | A   I believe so, sir.

3 | Q   Could you tell if shot three hit Mr. (Sharp) ?

4 | A   I couldn't tell if shot three hit him. I knew

5 | he fell backwards, but I couldn't tell if I had -- I

6 | didn't see any sort of wound that would indicate to me

7 | that -- that he had been hit.

8 | Q   So I know you said that you believed -- as

9 | Mr. (Sharp) brings his arms down from the parallel

10 | position, you believed he was swinging that gun in your

11 | direction. But would you agree you didn't know for

127

12 | sure?

13 | A   No. He was swinging it in my direction. He --
14 | he -- he was taking a classic shooter stance. He was
15 | stepping forward, the barrel was coming towards me. It
16 | was -- his hands were going towards the pistol grip. I
17 | believed that he was taking a shooter stance.

18 | Do I know exactly? I -- I'm not Mr. (Sharp) .
19 | But I know that that gun at that time was coming in
20 | my -- that barrel was coming in my direction aiming
21 | towards me, and his hands were going towards the pistol
22 | grip.

23 | Q   Okay. But it never actually pointed in your
24 | direction?

25 | A   It was coming -- it never -- it never pointed
1 | directly at me, no.

3 | Q   How much time would you say elapsed between you
4 | arriving at that corner, the southeast corner -- before
5 | you started cutting the pie, who much time elapsed
6 | between you arriving there and you firing your first
7 | shot?

8 | A   Seconds. Maybe five, six seconds, if even that
9 | much.

0 | Q   So, after you had fired your third shot, did
1 | you see Ms. (Sharp)   at this point?

2 | A   No, sir.

3 | Q   Could you hear her?

4 | A   No, sir.

• • •   The entire neighborhood said they heard
me screaming.

13   Q   To your knowledge, did Deputy (2)   see

14   Mr. (Sharp)   with his own eyes prior to you firing the

15   first shot?

16   A   No, sir, I don't know if -- I don't know if --

17   if Deputy (2)   -- I don't think so, but I don't know

18   for sure -- for sure.

19   Q   Do you have any reason to believe that he did

20   see Mr. (Sharp)   --

21   A   No.

22   Q   -- before you fired your first shot?

23   A   No. I believe I was the first one to see

24   Mr. (Sharp)   .

25   Q   Do you recall at what point Mister -- or, I'm

1   sorry -- Deputy (2)   took up that position on the other

2   side of the garage?

3   A   I don't recall.

3   So describe to me what happens after you fire

4   that third shot. Start with what Mr. (Sharp)   does.

5   You say he falls to the ground?

6   A   He falls backwards. So he's lying on his back.

7   His feet are to me. His head is away from me. His arm

8   is -- his left arm is outstretched, and he's got the

9   shotgun still in his -- kind of across his forearm and

10   onto his left hand.

The moment Patrick's hand let go of the vodka bottle, Deputy 1 began shooting.

14   But how does he get onto his back? Does he

15   fall straight back, does he --

16   A   He falls -- I believe he fell kind of straight

17   back. I don't -- I don't recall -- I can't remember if

18   he -- if he kind of stumbled back or if he fell back. I

19   don't really -- I just know that's kind of how he wound

20   up.

21   Q   That was my question.

22   Was it something where he kind of staggered a

23   little, staggered to the side, staggered backwards, then

24   fell, or he just fell straight back like if you

25   pushed -- pushed a big board over?

1   A   I don't think he fell just straight. I don't
2   think he -- like a big board. He may have -- his legs
3   may have came out from underneath him, and he just fell
4   backwards. I wasn't paying attention. At that point I
5   just saw him fall backwards. I wasn't watching how he
6   did it.

19   Q   All right. What do you do? Do you maintain
20   the same position, standing position with your gun
21   trained on Mr. (Sharp)   ?
22   A   I think I -- I think I kind of went down to a
23   knee for a second. I was just kind of in shock what had
24   just happened.
25   And everything was kind of -- you know, space
1   and time just seemed to -- almost like vertigo. So I
2   think I went down to a knee for a second.
3   I was still keeping my weapon pointed in the
4   direction. And then I stood back up.
5   And then I got back into position, because at
6   the time I didn't know -- I remember from my hunting
7   days when I was a little kid my dad teaching me that
8   sometimes animals will pretend to be wounded, and
9   they're just waiting for the moment to strike you, gore
10   you, before they can get away.
11   So I stood back up, and I re -- got a good
12   position and aimed right back at Mr. (Sharp)   and then
13   was just going to hold that position until other
14   deputies arrived at the scene, because I could hear

15 radio chatter, and I knew other people were going to be

16 en route.

9   Q   Did you believe you had -- either of your first

10 three rounds had struck Mr. (Sharp) ?

11   A   I didn't know, to be honest with you. I

12 couldn't see any -- the way -- I remember he was sweaty,

13 and the way the sun was glistening off his body, I

14 couldn't see any -- and I knew the entrance wounds would

15 be small. I couldn't see any entrance wounds.

16   And, since he was lying on his back, I couldn't

17 see any sort of exit. Any -- any sort of thing that

18 would indicate that there was an exit wound.

19   Q   Well, was there anything about the way he

20 reacted after you fired any of the first three rounds

21 that led you to believe you struck him?

22   A   No. I had no -- he didn't spin around, he

23 didn't -- he didn't grab at any sort of wound on his --

24 on his torso. I had no indication that -- whether I had

25 struck him or not.

1   Q   Beyond the fact that he had just fallen onto

2   his back.

3   A   He had fallen on his back.

4   Q   So was he moving at all while he was on his

5   back?

6   A   No, sir.

• • • He was never on his back. He spun around after he was shot and landed face down. The gun was nowhere within his reach.

13   Q   Okay. So, in your recorded interview, you said

14   that you could still see that Mr. (Sharp)   had control

15   of the shotgun in his hand while he was on his back on

16   the grass.

23   A   Exactly, yes, sir.

24   Q   So you also went on to say -- in your recorded

25   interview you said you weren't sure if the shotgun was

1   in his hand or close enough that he could reach it. You

2   could tell that the shotgun was near his left hand. You

3   could see the elongation of the gun. It was lying next

4   to his body.

24   So was it possible that the gun was not

25   actually touching his hand, that it was just close to

1   it?

6   I know it was by his hand. I know it was in a

7   way -- I wouldn't have been able to say that he would be

8   able to manipulate it. Grab it, yes. Manipulate it,

9   no.

11   So how long does it take for Mr. (Sharp)   to

12   get from a standing position to the position on his

13   back? Does he go right to his back?

14   A   I don't recall. It seemed like it was pretty

15   quick, but I don't -- I couldn't tell you how fast. It

16   wasn't -- it wasn't a staggered, slow movement. It

17   was -- it was relatively quick.

18   Q   Was he flat on his back, or was he partially on

19   his side?

20   A   He was flat on his back.

4   Q   So what happens at that point?

5   A   I get back. I take a knee real quick. I get

6   back up. Mr. (Sharp)   sits up quickly. The shotgun is

7   in his hand, and he's turning his body to put it into a

8   seated shooting position. And that's when I fire a

9   fourth round.

10   Q   So what do you mean he sits up? How does he

11   sit up?

12   A   He -- he's lying on his back. He just turns

13   his -- he like gets his arm underneath him, sits up, and

14   he -- with -- the shotgun is in his control, and he sits

15   up, and he tries to -- he's turning the weapon again

16   towards me.

17   Q   So he makes -- basically the same movement he

18   had made prior to you firing the first shot, he makes

19   that motion again, essentially?

20   A   Essentially. He's sitting -- he's laying --

21   although he's lying on his back, and he's -- he gets

134

These renditions show what it looked like right after he dropped the vodka bottle.

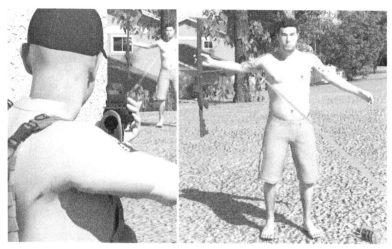

The shot that grazed him prior to the fatal one

Fatal shot

136

22 control of the shotgun.

23   And then he sits up, twists his body to sit up
24 to put the shotgun into a seated shooting position. I
25 don't know how else to describe it.

2   So in your recorded interview you said that he
3   sat up, had control -- still had control of the weapon,
4   and he started swinging in your direction again?
5   A   Yes, sir. It was the same general motion.
6   Q   Did you see how he got control of the shotgun
7   the second time?
8   A   I didn't see -- I didn't see his hand grab it.
9   His left hand. I wasn't -- I was more focused just on
10 his center -- on the center mass. I wasn't watching his
11 hands.
12   Q   So you didn't see his hand reach over and grab
13 the fore-end of the shotgun?
14   A   I didn't -- I didn't see his hand do that, no,
15 sir.

2   Q   So it's essentially you fire the fourth round
3   when Mr. (Sharp)   is in, basically, the same position as
4   the first. The only difference is now he's on the
5   ground sitting up rather than standing?
6   A   Yes, sir.
7   Q   And does the -- does the barrel of the gun get
8   to about the same direction -- or the same angle when
9   you fire this fourth round as it did when you fired the
10 first?

```
11      A    No.  I think this time it actually got to me.

12   I can't -- I can't recall.



18      Q    All right.  And did his right hand ever

19   actually touch the gun?

20      A    It went into the -- it went towards the pistol

21   grip.  I don't know if he got a full grip on the pistol

22   grip or not.

23           Again, I was focused more on the barrel and

24   where the barrel was going as opposed to his hands.



3       Q    So you would agree, though, that just holding

4    the gun by the left hand at the fore-end, you can't fire

5    it that way?

6       A    If it's coming towards me and I have a

7    belief -- and I believe that he's going to -- because I

8    can't -- I don't know what his right hand is doing,

9    yeah, I would still fire that weapon.  I still believe

10   there's a danger to me if the muzzle is coming towards

11   me.

12      Q    Okay.  I appreciate that.  But that wasn't the

13   question I asked.

14           My question was:  The way that he is holding

15   the shotgun with that left hand by the fore-end, he

16   can't fire it from that position.

17      A    On his back or --

18      Q    In any way.
```

19   So the way -- the way he's holding it prior to
20   you firing shot one or prior to you firing shot four
21   where he's holding the shotgun with his left hand by the
22   fore-end --
23   A   Right.
24   Q   -- he cannot fire it the way he is holding the
25   gun like that. Would you agree?
1   A   Yes, sir.
2   Q   He needs his right hand to either come over and
3   grab the pistol grip and the trigger, or he needs to
4   reposition his left hand to fire that weapon.
5   A   Yes, sir.
6   Q   All right.
7   And this second time before you firing shot
8   four, you never saw his right hand actually touch the
9   pistol grip?
10   A   No, sir.
11   Q   You never saw his right hand actually touch the
12   pistol grip before shots one or three; correct?
13   A   No, sir.
14   Q   And, as you sit here today, you don't remember
15   the barrel actually pointing in your direction for this
16   fourth shot?
17   A   I remember it coming in my direction. I can't
18   recall if it made it directly on me. His body momentum
19   was moving the barrel towards me.
20   Q   Okay.
21   And in your recorded interview you had said

139

22 after Mr. (Sharp)   sat up, he still had control of the

23 weapon, he started swinging it in your direction again

24 so you fired.

25   A   Yes, sir.

1   Q   So that would lead me to believe that the gun

2   didn't actually ever get into your direction; right?

3   A   It may have been. By the time I fire to the

4   time that he's continuing to swing, because it's a fast

5   motion, it may have.

6   But I may have already -- my round may have

7   already struck him at the point that the -- that the

8   barrel is facing directly at me.

9   Q   So did Mr. (Sharp)   actually ever sit all the

10 way up; that is, so his body is at a 90-degree angle?

11 Do you know what I'm saying?

12   A   I know what you're saying. I don't know what

13 angle -- he was sitting up. I can't -- I wouldn't be

14 able to tell if he was sitting up fully -- it looked

15 like he was sitting up fully because he was turning his

16 whole body. He was sitting up and turning his body

17 simultaneously to face me.

3   Q   So how long did it take him to sit up total?

4   Was that something that he did quickly? Did it take him

5   a couple of seconds?

6   A   It was quickly. It was -- I wasn't counting,

7   but it was very quick. It was shocking how fast.

140

19   Q   So can you estimate how much time elapses
20 between shots three and four?
21   A   I couldn't recall. Time seemed to be moving
22 really slow at this point. Like I said, I watched the
23 shell casings just slow motion out of the -- out of the
24 chamber of my rifle.

11   Q   So can you tell if this fourth shot strikes
12 Mr. (Sharp) ?
13   A   I can't tell. I don't see.
14   But the way his body -- as he's moving quickly
15 to turn towards me with the shotgun and then I fire, his
16 momentum, his body seems to go limp when he falls over
17 onto his stomach.
18   It looks like he probably got hit on that round
19 but, again, I can't tell, because I don't see any -- any
20 sort of indication that -- of a wound. I don't see
21 anything indicative of an exit wound.

6   And his arm -- I think one of his arms is kind
7   of underneath him. I think his right arm is still
8   underneath him, but his left arm is still kind of
9   cradling the shotgun. The shotgun is laying on the
10 grass, and his left hand is kind of cradled over the top
11 of it.

22   Q   But he's still -- his feet are still pointed in
23 your direction?

24   A   Yes, sir.

25   Q   And the shotgun is still touching him?

1   A   Yeah. He still had a -- his arm was -- his

2 hand was draped over it. He was still -- it was still

3 near his body.

12   I see a -- a female wearing a red -- I believe

13 it was a red sweater and black hair run from the area

14 over by the apartments. Over by the condos. I just

15 could see a figure dart out and run towards

16 Mr. (Sharp)   's body.

17   And then I -- me and (Dep. 2)-- me and Deputy

18 (2)   both start yelling at her to get back. And then

19 she -- she gets back or she leaves.

20   And then a few seconds later she goes running

21 back again, and we tell her again -- we're giving her

22 commands, "Get back. Get back."

23   Q   So you never saw Ms. (Sharp)   in that position

24 over by her house after contacting Mr. (Sharp)   ?

25   A   No. I never saw Mrs. (Sharp)   .

1   Q   But it's possible she could have been there?

2   A   She could have been. I never -- I never saw

3 her, though.

16   But I remember it was Mrs. (Sharp)   the second

17 time we were telling her to get back, that's when I kind

18 of saw Sergeant (4)   and Deputy (3)   coming from

19 my right field of vision.

15   Q   Does Ms. (Sharp)   ever get to Mr. (Sharp) 's

16   side?

17   A   Yes, sir.

18   Q   Is she actually on top of Mr. (Sharp) ?

19   A   I think the first time she kind of went

20 running towards him. I don't remember if she actually

21 made contact with him, and then we started calling her

22 back.

23   I think the second time is when she went over

24 and kind of like hugged him or cradled him or -- or held

25 on to his body.

1   And that's -- again, we were still -- because

2 we're trying to get back. We weren't -- I wasn't sure

3 if he was wounded, and I didn't know who this person was

4 at the time.

5   Q   How long was she there hugging him?

6   A   A second. Probably -- not very long. Maybe a

7 second, two seconds. We were trying to get her away

8 from -- from him.

17   Q   Did you ever actually see Deputy (2)   grab

18 Ms. (Sharp) ?

19   A   No. I didn't see Mister -- I didn't see Deputy

20 (2)   grab Ms. (Sharp)   .

7   Q   Could you tell that Mr. (Sharp)   had been hit

8 when you arrived at his side?

9   A   Yes, sir. I could see that there was an entry
10 wound.

11   Q   Was he still breathing at that point?

12   A   I couldn't tell. It looked -- I couldn't tell
13 if it was agonal breathing or if it was regular --
14 regular breathing.

15   Q   And what do you mean by "agonal breathing"?

16   A   Like a labored breath that -- it's just a
17 death -- a breath that somebody takes where your body is
18 just -- it looks like it's breathing. It's just in the
19 motions of breathing, but it's not actually taking in
20 air.

17   Q   So, at the time you contacted Mr. (Sharp)   , you
18 were not aware of what may have triggered his behavior
19 that day?

20   A   That would be correct, sir.

21   Q   At the time you contacted Mr. (Sharp)   , you
22 were not aware that Mr. (Sharp)   was despondent over a
23 recent marital issue?

24   A   I didn't know for sure. I didn't know that
25 that was the exact house.

1   Q   At the time you contacted Mr. (Sharp)   , you
2 were not aware that he had been drinking heavily for the
3 last several days?

4   A   I did not. I was not aware of that, sir.

5   Q   And, most importantly, at the time you
6 contacted Mr. (Sharp)   , you were not aware that he was

7   suicidal?

8   A   Not -- not upon initial contact, sir.

9   Q   Were you aware that Mr. (Warner) had informed

10   Deputy (2)   that he had had to talk Mr. (Sharp)   out of

11   committing suicide a day or so before?

12   A   I was unaware of that.

13   Q   Do you believe that this would have been

14   information that would have been helpful to you to have

15   known prior to contacting Mr. (Sharp)   ?

16   A   I believe the information would have -- it

17   would have been nice to know. I love getting as much

18   information as possible. I think it would have been of

19   benefit to get as much information as possible.

20   However, with the circumstances, still a 9-1-1

21   hangup call from inside of a residence and not knowing

22   what was occurring inside of that residence or what had

23   occurred inside that residence, having information about

24   what the subject wants to do or what has been in the

25   past is -- while it's relevant information, it's not

1   completely relevant to what may be happening at that

2   time.

9   Q   So why -- why could you not have stopped,

10   talked to Deputy (2) , talked to Mr. (Warner)   , got all of

11   this information, and in the meantime waited for

12   additional resources to arrive, set up a perimeter,

13   requested an air unit, and see if you can contact

14 | Mr. (Sharp)   that way?

15 | A   I wanted to -- with -- with the threat of

16 | somebody wanting to shoot through a door or shoot

17 | somebody that contacts them, while that person may at

18 | that time say they want -- that they're going to stay in

19 | that apartment or they're going to be in that apartment,

20 | at any time that person could leave.

21 | And with no fencing, no -- no -- around the

22 | area and a school close by, I didn't want a repeat of

23 | Sandy Hook. I didn't want to have -- I wouldn't have

24 | been able to live with myself if I had known that an

25 | armed homicidal gunman went towards and elementary

1 | school and started killing children.

● ● ●   Yet his own stray bullets came very
close to striking a 3-year-old child held
in his mother's arms.

4 | Q   So you're basing your response to the situation

5 | on what happened in Sandy Hook?

6 | A   I base my information -- my responses on all

7 | kinds of events, not just Sandy Hook.

8 | But we have an armed gun -- and we're close to

9 | a school. We have an armed gunman with what was

10 | described as a shotgun, but it could be a high powered

11 | rifle.

146

18   Why could you not have waited another two

19   minutes for additional deputies to arrive and have

20   requested an air unit?

21   A   I could have. But I made the decision not to

22   do that.

23   Q   But my question is: Is there anything that

24   prevented you from waiting an extra two minutes for

25   additional deputies to arrive, set up a perimeter, and

1   request an air unit?

2   A   Public safety.

3   Q   Can you explain?

4   A   I didn't want that armed gunman to leave that

5   home and start shooting people or make his way towards a

6   school and start shooting and killing children. I

7   wanted to have containment.

8   Two minutes is a long time for somebody that's

9   already made homicidal statements.

10   Q   Okay.

11   Well, you saying you didn't know where he was

12   is an argument for not advancing by yourself. He could

13   have been around any one of those corners, and him

14   seeing you could have set off a gun battle right there.

15   Would you agree?

16   A   Yes, sir.

17   Q   So what better way to get eyes on the situation

18   than to call ASTREA? Or ASTREA; right?

19   A   Mm-hmm. You can do that. It's -- it's one

20   option. But it's not the only option.

                              147

21   Q   All right.

22   But you do agree you could have waited for

23   additional resources two minutes for other deputies to

24   respond, set up a perimeter and call an air unit?

25   A   I could have made that decision, yes.

1   Q   So do you believe if you had had all of that

2   information that we just went through you would have

3   handled the situation any differently?

4   A   I would have done exactly the same thing that I

5   did. I wouldn't have done anything differently.

• • •   This cold-blooded statement compelled me to write this book.

6   Q   Even if you know that Mr. (Sharp)   was

7   essentially attempting to commit suicide?

8   A   Yes. Because at the time I still don't know --

9   we still have a 9-1-1 hangup call. We don't know who is

10   in that apartment. We don't know if there is somebody

11   dead or dying in there.

12   That only -- that only exacerbates, because

13   he's made a homicidal threat to somebody that came to

14   his door, and we don't know if his wife is still in

15   there. I don't know if the (Sharps)   have children.

16   Q   Well, that's my whole point.

17   Why not stop and talk to Mr. (Warner) ? He's a

18 family friend. He was the one that was just there
19 talking with Ms. (Sharp)   .
20   A   Right. I -- I -- I understand the option
21 you're presenting. That is one option.
22   However, my option is another option, to go
23 get -- and, in my experience of being in the military
24 and my training, having eyes on the location, having
25 something on the location as soon as possible, is also
1   as beneficial.

• • •   Marines are trained to kill. Is it because
         he didn't get to kill anyone when he was
         a Marine?

25   Q   So you don't think you could have set up a
1   perimeter and used a bullhorn to try to communicate to
2   him, talk to him for a minute, see what was going on?
3   A   If we had known what was going on, yes.
4   Once I had established contact, once I had
5   seen, getting eyes on -- on the apartment or the condo,
6   if I saw the subject still inside, then we would have
7   established a perimeter, and we would have gotten
8   contact.
9   However, if in that same scenario I start
10 hearing gunshot blasts south of my location, then I know
11 that individual has left his home, and now he's shooting
12 at people. So now I know -- I can hear where he is by

149

13 | the proximity of his gun blasts.

14 | Q   Did you ever hear a shotgun blast?

15 | A   No, sir.

16 | Q   Were you injured in any way as a result of this

17 | incident?

18 | A   No, sir.

19 | Q   I know that a lot of things are possible, but

20 | I'm trying to deal specifically in the information that

21 | you had at the time you made contact with Mr. (Sharp)   .

22 | Now, I don't -- personally, I don't see how

23 | Sandy Hook applies to this situation. You had no reason

24 | to believe that Mr. (Sharp)   was going to go to a nearby

25 | school and shoot anybody.

1 | A   It wasn't that he was. It was the proximity of

2 | the school.

3 | So you weren't treating this as a situation

4 | where you've got a suicidal person, somebody who is

5 | suffering from a mental health condition?

6 | A   I had no information that led me to believe

7 | that at that time.

8 | Q   Are you aware -- well, if you had stopped and

9 | talked to Deputy (2) and (Timothy Warner) , you would have

10 | known, "Hey, I had to talk him out of suicide a couple

11 | of days ago. He's been drinking ever since. He's

12 | trying to commit suicide."

13 | If you had stopped and talked to them, that's

14   information you could have gotten from them; right?

15   A   Yes, sir.

16   Q   So let's assume that you did stop and get that

17   information.

18   What is your training from the (Beach City)

19   Sheriff's Department with regard to approaching

20   situations involving individuals suffering from mental

21   health conditions?

22   A   Well, what we're taught is we're taught every

23   situation. You approach it first from an officer safety

24   standpoint.

25   You get to the scene, and you make sure that

1   there aren't any weapons that are going to hurt people

2   in play. That if the subject has a weapon, they need to

3   be disarmed, they need to put that weapon down, and the

4   scene needs to be made safe. That's always the first

5   thing that we're taught. Make the scene safe.

6   If the subject cooperates and puts their weapon

7   down and they're secured and detained, then we make an

8   assessment at that point whether PERT needs to be called

9   or -- if any sort of professional services need to be

10   provided for assessment.

11   But the first thing we need to do is make sure

12   the scene is safe.

13   Q   So, if you know you're dealing with somebody

14   who is suicidal and armed with a weapon, a gun, that

15   doesn't change your approach at all?

16   A   Well, if we know they're armed with a gun,

17 we're gonna -- we're gonna try and make -- give them

18 commands to put the weapon down.

19   Q   But the fact that they're armed with a gun and

20 suicidal or suffering from an acute mental health issue,

21 that doesn't change your approach or how you approach

22 contacting an individual at all?

23   A   No. I'm still gonna contact them from a

24 position of cover and concealment or cover and safety.

25   I'm gonna give them commands to put that weapon

1   down, and I'm gonna expect 100 percent compliance.

2   Q   So your No. 1 goal is officer safety?

3   A   Yes, sir.

4   Q   It's not the safety of the individuals you're

5   dealing with, the safety of the community at large? It

6   is solely officer safety?

7   A   Officer safety and the safety of the community.

8   Q   But it's officer safety first?

9   A   When we are call -- when we have a call, that's

10 what we -- that's what we focus on, making sure that the

11 scene is safe. Officer safety is always paramount, but

12 the safety of the public is equally as paramount. The

13 subject needs to cooperate.

14   Q   Okay. So is officer safety equal to the safety

15 of the community, or is officer safety paramount?

16   A   They're both equal. I would consider officer

17 safety to be equal to the safety of the public. I

18 wouldn't want anybody to get hurt. I wouldn't want any

19 officer to get hurt. I wouldn't want anybody in the

20 | community to get hurt.

21 | That's why I would want that person to drop

22 | that weapon and move away from it so we could secure

23 | it.

5 | Q Do you try to avoid situations in which you

6 | have to use deadly force?

7 | So, for instance, in this situation, you would

8 | agree that's a pretty densely populated area that you

9 | were interacting with Mr. (Sharp)   in.

10 | A Yes, sir. It's a densely populated area.

11 | Q You're surrounded by condos 360 degrees; right?

12 | A Yes, sir.

13 | Q And we've already established that a 223 round

14 | fired from an AR-15 travels a very long distance; right?

15 | A Yes, sir.

16 | Q And penetrates walls pretty easily.

17 | A Yes, sir.

18 | Q So, based on your belief that safety is the

19 | No. 1 rule, it sounds to me like you would try to

20 | approach situations in ways where you avoid having to

21 | use deadly force; that is, fire your AR-15 in that kind

22 | of situation.

23 | A You approach it in -- in a way that -- that

24 | best suits the situation.

25 | Sometimes you have to fire a weapon, and that's

1 | why you look for your backdrop. You try to understand

2 | what you're doing, and you try to assess your options at

3 that time.

4   If the person -- if the person -- if you give

5 commands -- in this scenario, if I give somebody a

6 command to put the weapon down, and they -- let's say a

7 gun -- and it's not pointing at me in any way, it's just

8 up in the air, he's just passive and he's not pointing

9 at me, he's just passively resisting me, I wouldn't

10 shoot him. I would hope that he would listen to my

11 verbal commands and put the weapon down.

● ● ●   So why did he shoot him then?

12   And if he says, "Hey, I'm gonna kill myself"

13 but he keeps that gun pointed up in the air away from me

14 and away from hurting anybody else, then it's still just

15 passive resistance.

16   I'm gonna take a position of cover, I'm gonna

17 call for additional units, and I'm gonna maintain that

18 scene.

19   However, if this individual makes a movement,

20 makes a furtive motion with that firearm towards me,

21 towards a member of the public, I will have to use my

22 firearm in defense of their life.

23   Q   Okay. I appreciate that, but it didn't really

24 answer my question.

25   A   I'm sorry.

1   Q   In responding to the situation, were you

2   actively looking for ways to avoid having to use your

3   AR-15?

7   I was going where I was going to try and get

8   eyes onto the apartment. So I had my AR-15 with me, but

9   I was hoping I would not have to use it.

• • •   It seems like he was looking for an excuse to use it.

10   Q   Well, you would agree that your background was

11   not, in fact, clear when you fired.

12   A   Well, there were homes back there, but there

13   was nobody behind -- there was nobody physically walking

14   behind me. Behind -- or behind Mr. (Sharp) .

15   Q   You're aware that two of your rounds struck

16   condos.

17   A   Yes, sir.

18   Q   One of them, thankfully, lodged in the exterior

19   of a condo, but another actually penetrated the wall,

20   went through a bed, went through a closet and came to

21   rest in a hallway.

22   A   Yes, sir.

23   Q   You're aware there were people home in both

24   residences?

25   A   That one I was aware of.

1   Q   Are you aware that there was a woman in her

2   backyard only feet away from where the round struck and

3   lodged in her -- in the exterior of her home?

4   A   No, sir. I wasn't aware of that.

5   Q   She actually saw the leaves falling from the

6   round coming through the trees in her backyard.

7   Looking back at that, do you think it probably

8   would have been better to have chosen an option that did

9   not necessarily require you to fire your AR-15 in that

10 situation?

11   A   No, sir. I would have still brought my AR-15.

12 It was the best weapon to have at the situation with

13 somebody armed with a shotgun.

14   Q   It sounds to me in looking at this like you had

15 made the decision that you were going to use your AR-15

16 before you even got out of your car. Is that a fair

17 assessment?

18   A   No, sir. I was gonna have my AR-15 with me

19 because it's the best tool for -- it's -- if somebody

20 has a long gun of unknown -- again, like I had mentioned

21 before, I don't know Mr. (Warner) and his experience with

22 firearms. So I don't want to be armed with a weapon

23 that's not at least equal to somebody that may be armed

24 with a high powered rifle themselves.

16   Q   So what's your familiarity with learning domain

17 37?

156

The trajectory from the shooter's AR-15 going through my neighbor's backyard during the time she was outside holding her three-year-old son.

18   A   What's the topic on learning domain 37? I'm

19   not really sure.

20   Q   Dealing with people with disabilities,

21   including mental disabilities.

22   A   I believe we took a class or we had some

23   training on that in the academy.

24   Q   So, prior to this incident, the last time you

25   remember receiving any training on this was at the

1   academy?

2   A   No, sir. I had a PERT class in February of

3   2014.

4   Q   All right.

5   And did that PERT class deal with the (Beach City)

6   Sheriff's Department's PERT protocol? That is, what the

7   PERT officers do, how to call the PERT team when you

8   need it, et cetera?

9   A   No, sir. It was more of a class of just

10   different types of mental disabilities and just how

11   to -- I don't want to say -- it was put on by -- I can't

12   remember if they were doctors or counselors.

13   But people have different -- just identify

14   different types of -- when you're out in the field

15   somebody that may be autistic or schizophrenic, things

16   along those lines.

17   Q   All right.

18   Did it teach you from a law enforcement

19   perspective how to approach situations in which you know

20   somebody is suffering from a mental health issue?

21   A   Not so much from a law enforcement perspective.

22   More from a therapeutic.

3   Q   How long was this training?

4   A   It was eight hours. It was an eight-hour

5   class. It was a one-day class.

7   Would you agree that, to the extent possible,

8   responding officers should observe the behavior

9   exhibited by a person in an effort to determine what is

10 happening and what might be prompting the observed
11 behavior?

18   THE WITNESS: I approach -- if I get a call,
19 again, officer safety, community safety. Officer
20 safety. If there's a weapon in play, the weapon gets
21 dealt with first.
22   At that point you treat it like any other call.
23 You go up, you talk to somebody, talk to a person, and
24 you make an assessment from there. If they need
25 additional resources, then we -- then we would call for
 1 them.

15   Q   Would you agree that peace officers must become
16 familiar with the behavioral and psychological
17 indicators of mental illness in order to determine if an
18 individual is a danger to others, danger to self, or
19 gravely disabled and determine an appropriate response
20 and resolution option?

24   THE WITNESS: I would agree that we should try
25 to assess somebody.

      • • •   But he didn't care about anyone except
                    himself.

13   Q   Would you agree that how peace officers respond
14   to persons living with a mental disorder can have a
15   tremendous impact on how these encounters will be
16   resolved?
17   A   Yes.
18   Q   Would you believe that the basic philosophy of
19   any law enforcement officer should be to respond in a
20   manner that is humane, compassionate, and supportive?

25   THE WITNESS: I would agree that we should be
1   professional and humane.
2   I guess I would also argue that it depends on
3   the call.   Depends on what kind of call we're getting.

14   Q   What about compassionately and supportively?
15   A   If the scene is safe, yes.   Everything is -- as
16   long as the scene is safe, then I would agree with
17   everything.
18   Q   All right.
19   Would you agree that a mental disorder creates
20   problems with feeling, thinking, and perception?
21   A   I think that might be beyond my scope of
22   training.
23   Q   Well, I pulled this straight out of learning
24   domain 37.

13   A mental disorder affects a person's behavior
14   by causing bizarre and/or inappropriate behavior.

19   THE WITNESS: Depending on the mental
20 condition, it may.

23   A mental disorder can be short term -- that is,
24 acute -- or long term, chronic?
25   A   I would agree with that, yeah.

1   Q   Finally, would you agree that officers must be
2 able to recognize general indicators of mental illness
3 so that appropriate actions can be taken?
4   A   I would agree with that.

16   What is (Beach City) Sheriff's Department's policy
17 and procedure with regard to contacting an individual in
18 the field who is suffering from the mental health
19 issue?
20   A   We would, again, assess the -- we would assess
21 the scene, make sure that the scene is safe, officer
22 safety, public safety.
23   Once that criteria is met, then contact the
24 subject, and you make a determination, ask them simple
25 investigative questions, conversation.
1   And if you start getting some of those
2 indicators, then you can call for additional assistance;
3 PERT, for example.
4   If they have in-home treatment, if they're --
5 if they're under the care of a physician, you try and

6   get as much of that information as possible.

7   You approach them in a way that, if you
8   recognize the fact that they're -- they suffer from
9   some kind of mental illness, you try and approach them
10 in a way where you can -- where they understand that
11 you're there to help them and not -- not cause them any
12 sort of -- any sort of -- try not to scare them, I
13 guess.

15   Any other tactical actions that you're
16 encouraged to use by (Beach City) Sheriff's Department
17 policy and procedure in regard to responding to
18 situations involving individuals with mental health
19 issues?

22   THE WITNESS: I don't think there's any sort of
23 tactical requirements. Generally, we have a contact
24 deputy and cover deputy.
25   But we -- we just call for additional resources
1   as we need them. Usually two people are dispatched to a
2   call, and then as additional resources are needed. But
3   you always take an approach, again, on the side of
4   officer safety.

7   What about seeking additional information?
8   A   You can do that if -- if you're responding to a
9   call and maybe their caretaker is there or a family

162

10 | member, if you know, if you're provided with the
11 | information, if you know the information that the person
12 | has a mental illness, then you can get that information
13 | and see if that -- if PERT can respond, you provide that
14 | information to PERT.
15 | If PERT can't respond, then you can try and
16 | take it upon yourself to do that or provide that
17 | information -- if you determine that they're so gravely
18 | disabled or a danger to themselves or others that you
19 | have to take them to the hospital, you provide that to
20 | the LPR facility once you get there.
21 | Q   And you're actually encouraged to do that by
22 | (Beach City) Sheriff's Department policy and procedure?
23 | A   You're encouraged.
24 | Q   But you did not seek additional information
25 | here before contacting Mr. (Sharp)   ?
1 | A   No, sir.
2 | Q   You're also encouraged to request backup
3 | because situations can be unpredictable and escalate
4 | quickly?

13 | Q   Is there any reason you could not have
14 | requested additional deputies there before you actually
15 | put eyes on their residence?
16 | A   At the time I could have. There's a lot of
17 | things I could have done.
18 | But, again, I wanted to get eyes -- I wanted --
19 | my plan was to do it the way I did it, and that's --

20 | that's how I was gonna go about doing that.

21 | Q   And you were not going to change your plan no

22 | matter what information you were presented with? Or no

23 | matter what (Beach City) Sheriff's Department policy and

24 | procedure is, that was your plan, and you were going to

25 | stick with it?

1 | A   No. My plan is always fluid. It changes. It

2 | changed when Mr. (Sharp)   was in the grass with the

3 | shotgun.

10 | Q   What about calming the situation? Are you

11 | encouraged to calm the situation?

12 | A   You're encouraged to calm the situation.

13 | However, you also have to look at the -- at the entire

14 | situation.

15 | Calming the situation down where somebody has

16 | nothing in their hands and they might be upset is very

17 | different than calming a situation down when somebody is

18 | upset and they have a shotgun in their hands, for

19 | example.

20 | There's -- calming the situation down means me

21 | giving commands and putting that shotgun down and

22 | following my orders explicitly, and that's calming the

23 | situation down.

24 | Q   Okay.

25 | Now, I know you didn't stop to talk to Mr.(Warner)

1 | or Deputy (2)   so you didn't know about

2   Mr.   (Sharp)'s -- the extent to which he was suicidal at

3   that point.

4   However, you said after seeing Mr. (Sharp)   in

5   the grass with the shotgun under his chin and him

6   saying, "Shoot me," you realized he was suicidal at that

7   point.

8   A   When he was standing up and he was -- had the

9   shotgun in his left hand. He was standing up saying,

10   "Shoot me."

● ● ●   Notice he didn't say yelling.

11   At that point I realized that he's -- this

12   person is -- yeah. He's -- he's -- he's goading me to

13   shoot him.

14   Q   Okay.

15   What efforts did you make, if any, to provide

16   reassurance that you were actually there to help him?

17   A   It was totally -- the only thing -- that comes

18   after the scene is safe. The scene isn't safe right

19   now. There's no -- there's only one way this has to go

20   right now, and that is putting that shotgun down.

21   The reassurance that we're here to help, the,

22   "Let me hear your side of the story," "What can we do to

23   help you," "Let's get some additional assistance here

24   for you," that comes after the shotgun is down on the

25   ground, and Mr. (Sharp)   is fully compliant with my

1   instructions.

2   Q   So you can't make any efforts to calm the

3   situation unless and until he puts the shotgun down?

6   THE WITNESS: Correct. He needs to put that

7   shotgun down.

8   (My Attorney) :

9   Q   Okay.

10   Well, let's assume you had stopped and talked

11   to Mr. (Warner) and Deputy (2) , and you knew the

12   background as to what had happened a couple of days

13   before. You knew that he had caught his wife cheating

14   on him.

15   If you had known that, when you see

16   Mr. (Sharp) , you know he's suicidal, you know he's been

17   drinking, you say, "Hey, man, listen, I understand

18   you've had a rough couple of days. I understand that."

19   You know, words to that effect. Calm voice. Isn't that

20   what you're trained to do?

21   A   Yes, sir.

22   Q   And you received training in active listening

23   as well; right?

24   A   Yes, sir.

25   Q   Is there a reason you could not have done that

1   here?

2   A   I didn't get a chance. My first, upon seeing

3   him, was I keyed up the microphone and said, "I see the

4   subject" and -- or "See the subject in the grass." He

5   stood up, and then he started yelling.

```
 6          So there was -- he -- he -- he -- based on what
 7    I was seeing, his demeanor was angry.  And angry with a
 8    shotgun.  So we're not just talking angry.  We're angry
 9    with a shotgun.
```

● ● ●   Actually I couldn't believe how calm
        (and brave) Patrick was.

```
10          I'm not gonna lower my weapon and get killed by
11    somebody who is angry about his wife cheating on him.
12    Q     Well, you believed that he was trying to goad
13    you into shooting him.
14    A     Yes, sir.
15    Q     You could have maybe not lowered your weapon
16    but certainly lowered your voice; right?
17    A     When I give commands, I want -- I want
18    everybody around -- I want my voice to travel as far as
19    possible.  I'm not gonna talk softly.
20    Q     Okay.  Well, that's actually the opposite of
21    what you're supposed to do when you're dealing with
22    somebody with a mental health issue; right?
```

```
 1    He's got a gun.  I have to give loud, verbal commands.
 2    He needs to put the gun down.
 3          At that point, once the scene is safe, I can go
 4    into, "Let's talk about this.  I understand you're
 5    upset."  But we didn't get to that point.
```

• • •   It didn't get to that point because he took
it upon himself to end my husband's life
without first trying to help him.

7   Q   Okay. Well, you're actually trained in
8   learning domain 37 -- and tell me if this is what you
9   remember -- move slowly. When possible, eliminate
10   emergency lights and sirens. Reduce environmental
11   distractions, such as radio noise. Assume a quiet,
12   nonthreatening manner when approaching and conversing
13   with the individual. If possible, avoid physical
14   contact.
15   I mean, is this what you're trained to do when
16   dealing with somebody with a mental health issue?

19   THE WITNESS: If possible. When possible.

21   Q   So you would agree, then, in this situation you
22   did not make any efforts to calm the situation? At
23   least insofar as learning domain 37 defines calming the
24   situation.
25   A   It wasn't possible. He had a shotgun.
1   Q   Learning domain 37 goes on to encourage you to
2   not make threats. Explicitly, it says, "Do not make
3   threats." Do not threaten the individual with arrest or
4   any other manner. Threats create additional fright,
5   stress, or potential aggression.
6   Is that what you remember from your training on

```
7    learning domain 37?

8        A    Yes, sir.

9        Q    So would you agree that screaming at

10   Mr. (Sharp)    to put the gun down is the exact opposite

11   of what learning domain 37 encourages you to do?


22       A    I believed he was going to shoot me.  He had

23   moved the shotgun into position and taken a shooting

24   stance.

25       Q    So you thought he was there to ambush an

1    officer?

2        A    I don't know what his intention was sitting in

3    the grass with the shotgun.  I don't know why he left

4    his condo.  I don't know what Mr.    (Sharp)'s intent

5    was.

6             I only hoped upon seeing him with a shotgun

7    that he would follow my verbal commands and put it down,

8    and that we would be able to talk this through and

9    resolve this peacefully.


21       Q    So, as a (Beach City) Sheriff's Department deputy,

22   you're trained to wait for appropriate assistance before

23   approaching a person who is potentially experiencing

24   psychiatric symptoms?

25       A    Right.  We would never contact somebody -- a

1    5150 by ourselves.  We always wait for another -- an

2    additional unit.
```

3   Q   What do you mean by "a 5150"?

4   A   Somebody -- a 5150 is somebody that has

5 mental -- it's a call that comes out of somebody that

6 maybe has a mental disorder.

7   Q   Okay. Somebody who is suicidal; right?

8   A   Or having an episode. Autistic, schizophrenic.

13   Q   So why is it important to wait for appropriate

14 assistance before contacting these individuals?

15   A   Safety. Officer safety.

16   Q   It's actually, you would agree, safer in these

17 situations to wait for backup before contacting them.

18   A   If you know that the subject -- if you know

19 that there is a subject to contact that might be that --

20 that has that potential, yes.

21   Q   So, if you had stopped and talked to Mr. (Warner)

22 and Deputy (2) , you would have known right at that

23 point before you ever even made contact with

24 Mr. (Sharp) that he was suicidal; right?

25   A   I would have known that Mr. (Warner) said that.

2   So now you're discounting what Mr. (Warner) said

3 with regard to whether or not Mr. (Sharp) is suicidal,

4 but you're putting a lot of credit in what he said when

5 it comes to whether or not Mr. (Sharp) pointed a

6 shotgun at him.

7   A   Right. It's -- you want to get -- you want

8   to -- you want to -- Deputy (2)   is getting that

9   information. He's -- he's the one conducting that part

10 of the investigation. So he's gaining all that

11 information.

12   And I'm going by what Deputy (2)   is taking

13 as -- as what -- what's coming across. I'm not gonna --

14 I'm not gonna interview Mr. (Warner) while Deputy (2) is

15 interviewing Mr. (Warner).

16   Q   But you don't know what Mr. (Warner) told Deputy

17 (2) because you didn't stop and ask him.

18   A   Correct, sir.

19   Q   So, if you had, you would have known

20 Mr. (Sharp)   was suicidal. And at that point would this

21 training have kicked in, and you would have considered

22 waiting for appropriate backup before contacting

23 Mr. (Sharp)   ?

1   THE WITNESS: No, sir. I would have done

2   everything exactly the same way I just did.

● ● ●   This guy seems to be the one with
            the mental disorder.

4   Q   Even though you're trained to wait for

5   appropriate assistance before approaching persons who

6   are potentially experiencing psychiatric symptoms?

171

10   A   You approach it just like any other pedestrian
11   contact. You usually -- if you know you're gonna be
12   approaching a subject that has those issues, then you
13   approach it in the same contact and cover situation.
14   Make the scene safe. One person does the contact while
15   the other person covers you to make sure that the scene
16   remains safe.

18   So you are encouraged in all calls to put
19   together a tactical plan before making contact?
20   A   Not a tactical plan. Make -- at least talk
21   about what may -- what may happen if you're gonna
22   contact a person. Find out, you know, who -- who's
23   gonna be contact, who's gonna be cover.

10   And is the reason you do this for officer
11   safety, safety of the public?
12   A   It can be. Sometimes it's better for -- for
13   the individual that you're contacting. If they're
14   more -- if they've had bad experiences with a particular
15   deputy, then it's probably better if the other deputy
16   that they haven't had a bad experience maybe be the one
17   that talks.

• • •   He didn't want to talk. He just wanted
to shoot.

172

```
21   Q   But you didn't form a plan here in this case.

22   A   I formed a plan.

23   Q   But you didn't form a plan with Deputy (2)  .

24   A   No, sir. I told him what I was going to do.
```

• • •   He formed a plan that he was going to
shoot his AR-15 that day.

```
1           Well, his testimony was different than that.

2    But your testimony today is that you told him you were

3    going to put eyes on the house?

4    A   Yes, sir.

5    Q   He didn't know -- he testified he didn't know

6    what you were doing, and he was surprised to see you at

7    the corner of that garage contacting Mr. (Sharp)  .

8    A   I was surprised to be contacting Mr. (Sharp)  ,

9    too.

10   Q   Don't you think it would have been better to

11   have stopped and talked to Deputy (2)    and discuss

12   these potentialities? "Hey, I'm gonna advance. Can you

13   cover me from this position? Or do you want to come

14   with me and cover me?"
```

```
23   Q   What were you going to do if you, in trying to

24   put eyes on the residence, you actually contacted the

25   individual with the shotgun? What was your potentiality

1    for that?
```

2   A   To handle it exactly how I handled it.

3   Q   And did you let Deputy (2) know that that's

4   how you were going to handle it if you came across that

5   potentiality?

6   A   No, sir.

7   Q   So when was the last time you received any

8   training from (Beach City) Sheriff's Department regarding

9   de-escalating situations?

10   Or have you ever received any training from

11 (Beach City) Sheriff's Department on how to de-escalate

12 situations?

13   A   Nothing -- I don't recall any sort of training

14 that's specifically about de-escalating situations. I

15 don't remember any sort of classes specifically with

16 that.

17   Q   So, as you sit here today, you can't think of

18 any training you've ever had as a (Beach City) Sheriff's

19 Department deputy regarding situation de-escalation?

20   A   I don't recall.

21   Q   So please describe your department's policy on

22 use of lethal force.

25   A   It would be aggravated active aggression.

1   That's where an individual is displaying behavior or a

2   weapon that's gonna cause great bodily injury to

3   somebody.

174

6   Q   Let me be more specific.

7   What does (Beach City) Sheriff's Department policy

8   and procedure say about when a deputy can use lethal

9   force?

10   A   When they feel that their life or the life of

11   somebody else may be in danger, either be killed or

12   seriously injured.

13   Q   Is it just when they feel that? Is it a

14   subjective standard?

15   A   They have to have a belief. Behavior displayed

16   that leads them to believe that somebody is going to --

17   that the subject is going to cause them to be killed,

18   the deputy, or a civilian.

19   Q   So, as far as your understanding is, at least

20   at the time of this incident, it was just a subjective

21   belief?

22   A   You had to have an action. Not a belief. You

23   had to have an action. You believed because the subject

24   was doing something, that led you to believe that.

25   Pointing a weapon, advancing on you with a knife, trying

1   to drive a car into you. There had to be an action

2   associated with the belief.

21   Q   Would you agree that deadly force is the

22   highest level of force an officer can use?

23   A   Yes, sir.

24   Q   Would you agree that special rules apply for

25   the use of deadly force as opposed to the use of less

                              175

1 lethal force?

2   A   Yes, sir.

3   Q   What are these special rules?

4   A   The subject has to be displaying a behavior,

5 and the deputy has to believe -- the law enforcement

6 officer has to believe that their life or life of

7 somebody else is in danger in order for them to use

8 deadly force.

23   Would you agree that deadly force can only be

24 used in immediate defense of life.

25   A   Yes, sir. I would agree with that.

1   Q   Would you agree that deadly force must be a

2 last resort?

3   A   If -- if none -- if none of the other options

4 are -- fit, yes, deadly force is -- is the last.

5   Q   So you're only to use deadly force when all

6 other force options are either ineffective or

7 impractical?

8   A   Impractical. Ineffective I wouldn't -- I

9 wouldn't use -- if somebody -- an example, I wouldn't

10 use what I would use -- I wouldn't use a -- I wouldn't

11 use a passive resistance with somebody that's displaying

12 acts of aggravated aggression. It wouldn't be

13 appropriate.

14   Q   All right.

15   Would you agree that deadly force can only be

16 used in the direst of circumstances?

9   Q   You would agree that deadly force is force
10   likely to cause death or great bodily injury?
11   A   Yes, sir.
12   Q   You would agree that as a law enforcement
13   officer you must show a reverence for life?
14   A   Yes, sir.
15   Q   And you would agree as a law enforcement
16   officer you can only use deadly force when no other
17   reasonable measures are available?
18   A   Yes. I would agree with that.
19   Q   You would agree that you can only use deadly
20   force when all other reasonable measures are exhausted?
21   A   I wouldn't agree with that.
22   Q   No?

3   THE WITNESS: There's a lot of situations where
4   other -- I would never use other methods before going to
5   deadly force.

● ● ●   Did he forget that he is now a Deputy
           Sheriff, not a Marine?

7   Q   Would you agree that you should give a warning,
8   when feasible, that deadly force will be used?
9   A   When feasible, yes.
10   Q   Would you agree that as a law enforcement

177

11 officer you are responsible for every shot?

12   A   Yes, sir.

21   Would you agree that an officer's subjective

22 fear is insufficient to justify the use of deadly

23 force?

1   THE WITNESS: It would have to accompany an

2 action. You can hold -- you can hold a gun to your

3 head, and I can be afraid that you might point it at me.

4 But without you actually attempting to point it at me, I

5 wouldn't shoot you.

7   Q   Okay. I understand your answer, and it's not

8 quite what I'm asking. So let me see if I can ask it a

9 different way. Well, let me ask it again with some

10 explanation.

11   You would agree that an officer simply being

12 afraid that somebody is going to kill them or cause them

13 great bodily harm is not enough to justify use of

14 force?

15   A   I would agree with that.

16   Q   You would agree that overreaction is excessive

17 force?

9   Are you trying to go higher -- a higher level

10 if somebody -- if somebody's exhibiting passive

11 resistance and then using what I would use for
12 assaultive behavior? Is that what you're talking about
13 overreacting?

14   (My Attorney) :

15   Q   Yes. Using more force than is called for in
16 any specific situation is excessive.

17   A   Yes, sir.

18   Q   So is it possible that your decision to charge
19 ahead and contact Mr. (Sharp)   on your own created the
20 necessity to use force?

10   THE WITNESS: No, sir. Mr. (Sharp)   had the
11 option to put the shotgun down when I gave him verbal
12 commands. He decided not to follow those instructions.

13   (My Attorney) :

14   Q   Well, he was also a .28.

15   So, as we sit here today, we don't really know
16 if he understood what you were telling him; right?

19   THE WITNESS: I hoped he would have understood
20 what I said.

22   Q   Would you agree at least that if you had
23 stopped at Deputy (2)   's location, gotten all of the
24 information, waited for backup to arrive, called an air
25 unit, it certainly wouldn't have hurt the situation or
1 made it any more dangerous?

5   THE WITNESS: I don't -- I don't think it would

6   have mattered one bit. The situation was dangerous

7   regardless.

17   Would you agree that, in doing what I just

18   suggested, there was a chance that you wouldn't have had

19   to have deployed your AR-15 in that situation, during

20   which you struck two residences, and only by the grace

21   of God there wasn't somebody laying in that bed when

22   your round went through it?

2   THE WITNESS: I don't know -- I don't know what

3   Mr. (Sharp)   would have done with his shotgun. I don't

4   know if I would have -- if anything different would

5   have -- would have occurred.

6   He -- he was the variable. Him leaving the

7   home was the variable with that shotgun.

8   (My Attorney) :

9   Q   Could it have hurt to have tried something

10   else?

11   A   It -- it was -- there were a lot of other

12   options to use. I -- I chose the best option that I

13   believed to be the best option at the time.

15   Looking back now, though, with -- obviously,

16   hindsight is 20/20. Looking back now are there any

17   options that you would have at least liked to have tried

180

18 before taking the option that you ultimately took?

19   A   No.

22   THE WITNESS: I would have done everything the

23 same.

● ● ●   His own pride is more important than a
         human life.

25   Q   You'd do it the exact same today knowing

1 everything you know?

2   A   Yes. I would have done it the exact same. I

3 would have -- would have -- with or without additional

4 information, I still would have went up to get eyes on

5 the apartment. That's what I would have done. That's

6 training that's followed me since the Marine Corps.

7   And I would have hoped that Mr. (Sharp) would

8 have followed my instructions. I would have hoped that

9 he hopefully would have just stayed in the apartment and

10 that we could have opened up a line of communication

11 with him. We could have contained him in there and

12 ultimately just waited him out to have a peaceful

13 resolution to this.

14   Q   Even knowing that he was suicidal, he had a

15 history of mental health issues, depression, and that he

16 was a .28, you still would do everything the exact same

17 way you did?

THE WITNESS: I would.

• • • Patrick likely saved future innocent lives that would have been lost at this deputy's capricious indiscretions.

21 Q   So please describe -- so you just said "suicide

22 by cop." What did you mean by that term?

23 A   It's a term that I've heard where individuals

24 will approach law enforcement, they'll display

25 aggravated acts of aggression, they'll point weapons at

1 police officers, they'll charge police officers with

2 weapons, they'll -- they'll try and get the police

3 officer -- or get they'll get the police officer to

4 shoot them because they don't want to -- they don't want

5 to commit suicide themselves. They don't want to do it

6 themselves. They don't want to pull the trigger or they

7 don't want to cut their wrists. They don't want to jump

8 off a cliff.

• • • So this means if someone asked a cop to slit their wrists, they'd do that for them? A strange contradiction of terms.

9   They'd rather have somebody else do it for

10 them. So they pick police officers because they know

11 that, if they charge us or if they kill one of us, that

```
12   they're going to be -- that if they commit another act
13   of aggression, if they shoot one of us and then go point
14   a weapon at another officer, they're going to get shot.
15          If they point a weapon at us, and we think --
16   we have the belief that our life is in danger, we're
17   going to shoot them.
18   Q     Have you received any training from the
19   Sheriff's Department in how to deal with situations
20   where you believe somebody is trying to commit suicide
21   by cop?
22   A     No, sir.
23   Q     Do you think that would have been helpful in
24   this situation?
25   A     No, sir.
1    Q     Do you believe if Mr. (Sharp)   wanted to harm a
2    law enforcement officer he would have sat in an open air
3    environment like he did and try to ambush officers
4    there?


8    Q     Did that seem like a good place to sit if you
9    were going to ambush officers?


11          THE WITNESS:  Yeah.  I mean, he could have.  I
12   don't know Mr. (Sharp)   's level of -- I don't know
13   Mr.  (Sharp) 's -- if he has any military training.  I
14   don't know what he was thinking.  I don't know -- again,
15   at the time I don't know anything about Mr. (Sharp)   .
```

This isn't a battlefield. It is a residential neighborhood.

• • •

10   Q   And so a lot of your response to this situation
11 was based on your lack of information about Mr. (Sharp)
12 and the situation that had led him to be in the grass
13 that day with the shotgun?

15   THE WITNESS: No. My response was based on the
16 information that I was provided by Sheriff's dispatch
17 and provided by Deputy (2)   at the scene.
18   (My Attorney) :
19   Q   Which was very little. Would you agree?

21   THE WITNESS: I wouldn't agree. It was enough
22 to make a decision.

24   Q   So why did you not deploy any less lethal
25 options in responding to Mr. (Sharp)   ?
1   A   He had a shotgun.
2   Q   Can you not use a less lethal shotgun in that
3 situation?
4   A   Only if I load it up with -- with lethal
5 rounds. He has a shotgun. I was not going to use
6 pepper ball or a bean bag against somebody that's going
7 to shoot me with either a slug or buckshot.

13 Q   And you already testified he never actually
14 pointed the shotgun at you. You believed he was moving
15 the barrel of the shotgun in your direction; right?
16 A   Yes, sir.
17 Q   So, when he's standing there with his arms out
18 parallel, could you not have shot him with a less lethal
19 shotgun at that point?
20 A   I could have. But, in my experience, less
21 lethal shotguns don't incapacitate somebody beyond the
22 point of being able to return fire with a weapon of
23 their own.
24   It's like being hit with a fastball. And we're
25 trained to shoot somebody in the midsection. So, if you
1   can take a punch, if you can take a fastball to your
2   chest, you can return fire with your own shotgun.

7   So you've got four rounds to see if you can
8   incapacitate him at the point where he's holding the gun
9   by the slide, out away from his body, parallel to the
10 ground with the barrel in the air; right?
11 A   Mm-hmm. Yes, sir.
12 Q   Why was that not an option?
13 A   Because I didn't -- I didn't bring it with me.
14 I didn't bring it with me.
15   And, if he gets hit, he can still fire. It
16 might not have stopped his motion. It's a less lethal
17 option. He's got a lethal shotgun. I have a -- a less
18 lethal alternative isn't -- isn't the appropriate use --

19   or piece of equipment to bring at that time.

20   Q   You've always got lethal backup; right?

21   A   It's a -- it's the -- an AR -- or a Glock .22

22   isn't -- the sight arrangement on that isn't as

23   effective as the longer sighting on the -- of the AR.

24   Q   So you don't think you could have been

25   effective from your vantage point with your side arm?

1   A   Not as effective, no.

24   Q   So regularly you're shooting your handgun on a

25   25-yard range.

1   A   From a distance of 15 yards maximum usual --

2   usually.

3   Q   You don't ever -- so it's your testimony today

4   under oath that you don't ever shoot at the range with

5   your Glock on a 25-yard range?

6   A   I do shoot on a 25-yard range. However, I am

7   not -- to qualify in the Sheriff's Department, we don't

8   have to qualify from the 25-yard distance.

1   I normally bring my AR-15 when I'm going to

2   shoot from a farther distance than 15 yards.

3   Q   Were you ever -- did any of your supervising

4   officers ever raise any concerns with you about

5   deploying your AR-15 in that area?

6   A   No, sir.

7   Q   You were never talked to by anybody at the

8   Sheriff's Department concerning your decision to deploy

9 your AR-15 in that area?

10   A   No, sir.

11   Q   Do you know if there were any changes to (Beach

12 City) Sheriff's Department policy and procedure or

13 training protocols after this incident?

14   A   Not that I'm aware of, sir.

● ● ●   I *know* that there was.

15   Q   Not as it pertains to the deployment of AR-15s

16 in urban settings?

17   A   No, sir.

18   Q   Or residential settings? I'm sorry.

19   A   Not that I'm aware of, sir.

20   Q   Was there a reminder bulletin put out

21 following this incident about your background or your

22 field of fire in deploying your AR-15 in residential

23 areas?

24   A   I don't recall, sir. There may have been, but

25 I don't recall.

2   In your interview you said that there was this

3 briefing that you had purportedly received a few days

4 before this incident about another officer being killed

5 at a 5150 call.

6   Do you remember anything about that?

7   A   I think that was one -- I think it was in

8   another state or something like that. Or -- I remember

9   there being some kind of call. I can't recall the

10   specifics because so many officers have been killed in

11   the past two years, and I seem to hear about all of

12   them. So after a while they all start blending

13   together, whether it be 5150 or domestic violence, gang

14   members. It's -- I can't remember any specifics.

25   Q   So is it fair to say as you sit here today you

1   don't remember really anything about this incident?

2   A   They've all blended. I don't know what

3   specific incident. They all blend together after a

4   while.

> • • •   It's not an everyday occurence that he
> deploys his AR-15 and kills someone.
> How does that blend in?

18   Q   And you did a walk-through later in the day

19   back at the scene.

20   A   Yes, sir.

21   Q   Now, you were able to talk to an attorney

22   before doing that walk-through?

23   A   Yes, sir.

24   Q   Did the attorney suggest to you anything to say

25   during the walk-through or raise any issues -- tell you

1   things not to say during the walk-through?

```
2     A    No, sir.

3     Q    What about during the interview?  Did the

4  attorney suggest to you things to say or things not to

5  say?

6     A    No, sir.
```

   • • •   And thus ends a condensed
summary of contradictions and
false statements.

CHAPTER 16

The red dot glowed on the voice recorder the entire time I was being detained—from 10 in the morning until 4:30 that afternoon.

I was shuffled from one deputy's office to another. There was a certain coldness about it that seemed totally inappropriate for what I was going through. *I didn't kill anyone!* I had just witnessed one of them murder my husband, and how that affected me just didn't seem to matter to them. I was surrounded by a bunch of people that seemed to care more about crafting a cover-up.

The first deputy's office I was dropped into was totally arrogant. He asked me random questions that had nothing to do with what I had just witnessed. He wouldn't answer any of the questions I asked him. I wanted to know if he knew my ex-husband. I told him my ex-husband worked at this exact same station, and was awarded two years straight for making more DUI arrests than any other law enforcement officer in the entire state of California— and that if *he* were the deputy at that liquor store last night when Patrick was buying that big vodka bottle, he would have followed him and arrested him for sure, and that Patrick would be in jail right now on DUI charges instead of dead.

The deputy wouldn't reply to that. By all of his efforts to distract me there is no way that he could rescind the fact that I just saw one of his colleagues murder my husband right before my eyes. Perhaps trying to distract me is a trained strategy. But it didn't work. He should have been a grief counselor, not an asshole.

I told him I had to use the restroom. He wouldn't let me use the women's restroom for some reason, so he escorted me to a jail cell, waiting outside for me to finish. Well at least it was clean, but it certainly wasn't private, and even through my tears it made me wonder why I was being treated like a criminal.

I couldn't help but wonder if the way they acted toward me was because they had worked with my ex-husband and knew of his bitterness about our divorce. When Patrick and I were first married, Patrick told me that my ex was following him around in his patrol car. When my daughter asked her dad about it, his reply to her made it pretty clear that he wanted to arrest Patrick for something. Patrick ended up filing a complaint. His sister, at the time being a sergeant in the Police Department, put an inquiry into this behavior with the Sheriff Internal Affairs. The stalking immediately stopped. Though at the time of the shooting my ex was a sergeant in a different precinct, I can almost be sure that he lauded all of his buddies' atrocious actions that day.

The sheriffs likely assumed that I was so upset that I wouldn't remember things in so much detail. Fueled by anger and injustice, I promptly wrote everything down as soon as I could after it happened. The details of that day are forever transcribed in my mind.

Why were several hours of my voice recording missing from the tape that the defense presented as evidence—when I *saw* the recording light *ON* the entire time? Isn't tampering with evidence illegal? I guess nothing is illegal if you're a cop.

I told them that Patrick was so depressed that sometimes he said he wanted to die. They kept statements like that in. But they left everything that I said that I saw them do wrong out of their "evidence". I'm positive I said some things that they didn't like. I knew a little more about them than most civilians because I used to be married to one of them. One of them that these guys actually *knew*. What a strange irony.

I remember saying to them, "I know for a fact there isn't much for you guys to do around here except check out the surf. So you use my husband for target practice because you're bored?" I could tell that really pissed them off, and of course that statement was missing from the recording.

They were trying to get me on something, and the worst thing they could use against me was my affair. I remember looking straight into one of the the detective's eyes and said: "If your spouse didn't give you sex for over a year and a half what would *YOU* do?" He didn't answer. I still remember the look on his face.

I told them about one of their deputies in the liquor store the night before who had watched my obviously intoxicated husband walk out with a big bottle of vodka and then get into his car and drive away. I said "I know that you know (my ex). *He* would have *NEVER* let someone even suspected of being drunk get into their car and drive away!" They never admitted to knowing my ex, but I was positive that they did.

They kept asking the same questions over and over again. I kept telling them over and over again the same things, because they were the facts. It was almost like they were trying to get me to change my story. I couldn't change my story because *the truth doesn't change.* Were they trying to manipulate me into saying things they'd rather hear instead?

They kept asking me, **"Did Patrick point the gun at the deputy? Was Patrick sitting or kneeling on the grass?"** I replied, "No, Patrick was standing motionless on the grass in a cross position the entire time before he was shot. Across from Deputy 1, I saw Deputy 2 aiming his rifle at Patrick also. *If Patrick was such a threat to their safety, why didn't Deputy 2 shoot him too?"*

"Did Patrick ever physically abuse you? Did he ever point a

gun at you or threaten to shoot you?" I replied, "No, not *ever*. We only played with the guns when we were acting out *Pulp Fiction* scenes in our house, and the guns weren't loaded." They already knew that in all of the twenty years we lived there that there had never before been a call dispatched to our address until that week.

"Were you planning on getting a divorce?" I replied, "No, he begged me to come back home two nights ago! We decided we were going to work it out. We even started making travel plans. I don't think someone who was planning on dying the next day would be making travel plans."

"How did you know the gun was jammed?" I replied, "I don't know, but just somehow *KNEW* that it was. Maybe *I willed it to be jammed*." To this day, I still can't answer that question in a way that would satisfy anyone who did not believe in supernatural occurences.

I emphatically said to them more than once, **"Patrick was just crying out for help. He was never going to shoot anyone! I really don't think he thought you guys would actually shoot him! THIS IS ALL WRONG. EVERYTHING YOU PEOPLE DID TODAY WAS WRONG!"**

Around noon I was escorted to another uniformed babysitter's office and had to walk barefoot for a distance on newly paved black asphalt. Then I had to run because my feet started to burn, which made the deputy run after me. Once I started to run, I felt a familiar freedom—what I was so used to running away from before, why I had been a marathon runner—*to get away from control freaks*. I wanted to keep going and run home, no matter how hot the ground was. There was no reason whatsoever why I needed to remain there. I didn't do anything wrong, *they* did. I didn't need to hang out in their facility partly clothed for hours on end just for their convenience. But at the time, I was too devastated to act on any of these thoughts.

It was around 2 pm, and I was being babysat by yet another deputy. I was resting my head on my arms criss-crossed on a table, staring down at the floor. I was very worried about my dogs, and wanted to comfort them. I needed to go home.

As I stared down at the floor, the carpet started to shimmer with grayish-white transparent wavy lines. I thought it was just what I was seeing through my tears. It seemed like some sort of energy field. I looked away, looked back, and it was still there. Patrick all of a sudden said to me, "This is SO COOL!" I could see him in my mind. I could feel him passing by me, like a breeze. Out loud I retorted, "WELL THIS ISN'T!" The deputy sitting nearby said, "What did you say?" I mumbled, "Never mind, forget it." This was the first thing Patrick said to me after he passed over. There was no way I could have been imagining this, because I was so completely distraught and dulled out to everything, barely surviving in an innate self-preservation mode.

I had to get home to my dogs, especially Emo who was in the car inside our garage only a few feet away from the shooter, witnessing the sound of someone killing his beloved owner. I know he suffered terribly when he heard the gunshots, so loud I can't imagine how that would be to a dog. Then he heard me screaming. I knew that he was traumatized. His hearing was never the same after that, and neither was he.

I was thirsty, and steady streams of snot kept running down my face. I used my tshirt. I wasn't offered anything to eat all day except by one deputy who was courteous enough to ask if I wanted a granola bar. I told him I just needed water. For a moment I thought I saw a hint of empathy in his eyes. I silently thanked him for being human.

The detectives who wanted to question me finally arrived. Though they were in plain clothes, they were just as presumptuous as the guys in uniform. They asked me the same questions over and over again for several hours. It was almost like they were trying to get me to change my story, to say something that they would rather hear, something that didn't make them look like they fucked up so badly. Understandibly the uniforms band together to protect their reputations. But I couldn't appease them. I saw everything, indelibly catalogued into my memory forever.

After the overly redundant interrogation, I was led to a small room where they took detailed photos of my face, arms, hands, and legs. I started to think they were going to ask me to take off all of my clothing. I asked them why they were doing this. They said the photos would indicate any signs of physical abuse. I told them it was *them* who were abusing me.

After I had told my attorneys of my experience in detainment, they thought my civil rights were violated. But I told them that this wasn't about me, and that they don't even need to bring up my captivity. I just wanted them to focus on the tremendous injustice done to Patrick.

When I listened to the tapes the sheriffs submitted as evidence, it was clear that they had omitted all of my incriminating statements, especially this one: **"I'm not completely certain what your training is but I AM SURE that you guys did EVERYTHING WRONG! It seems like you're more interested in protecting yourselves! Do you really fire an assault rifle in the middle of a residential neighborhood? Why was my husband wasted like an enemy on the battlefield? Did your deputy just come back from the war or something? What is wrong with you people?! Patrick never even came close to pointing the gun at anyone! He** was just depressed and sad. Do you murder someone just because they are depressed? Why didn't anyone try to counsel him first and say something like, 'Dude you don't have to do this' or whatever? I know why! Because your trigger-happy deputy couldn't wait to use his gun on somebody!!!"

I knew that they knew they fucked up.

CHAPTER 17

After the almost invasive photographs, they told me I could leave. I was given a landline and I called my daughter. At 4:30 in the afternoon, she was finally allowed to pick me up.

When she burst through the front door of the sheriff's station, I felt immeasurable comfort, knowing that this person loved me, when I hadn't before been allowed to be with anyone who gave a shit about what I had gone through that entire day. She was physically shaking. She glared at the uniforms alongside me, we hugged quickly, and I basically ran out the door with her. I couldn't wait to get out of there. We went to her car but she couldn't start driving right away. My daughter was doing the best she could as a twenty-three-year-old to be strong for me. It took several minutes for us to stop crying before either of us could speak.

She already knew everything. One of her dad's buddies at the station wasted no time in calling him to tell him about it. Right after that her dad called her. She told me everything his sheriff buddy said that had happened. They already had their cover-up story scripted. She said she didn't believe it because she knew Patrick wouldn't kill anybody.

She desperately wanted to know what *really* happened. The only words I could say between catching my breath while crying was that Patrick was dead—that I saw everything and that they killed him for no reason. I couldn't really talk. I was crying so hard I couldn't breathe. My voice was so hoarse that it hurt my throat to talk. We were both sobbing uncontrollably. After about ten minutes she started driving to my house.

We could not get onto my street. It was all taped off. I couldn't go into my house. The surrounding neighborhood was barricaded with cop cars and news reporters. My daughter got out of the car and walked through all of them, ducking under the yellow tape, over to the house. She wasn't afraid of the sheriffs; she knew most of them pretty well.

She came back several minutes later, saying that she got to see the dogs and take them out, but said a lot of detectives were in my house going through things inside. The scene upset her. I knew she was trying to hold back her tears.

They had somehow got a warrant to search my house. For what? Maybe because they know they screwed up very badly and hoped to find an excuse for their actions after the fact, by perhaps finding illegal guns or drugs or something like that inside my house? There wasn't anything there, not even inside the safe (had they been able to see its contents) that they could possibly use to vindicate their wrongdoing.

When I was finally allowed to go inside my house, it was almost 10:30 that night. I was waiting inside and around my daughter's car for six hours. My mom and dad had since arrived to be with me. I didn't want anyone close to me to see how horrible this was. I didn't want anyone else to suffer or to worry. I almost rather that they had not been there, even though I needed them to be. The whole thing just sucked.

Inside my house it looked like a much larger mess than it was before I left. Everything was torn apart like a robbery had taken place. As a matter of fact, I *was* robbed—one of them just took my husband away from me forever—for no reason at all.

All of our computers were gone, which I really needed for work. I had to beg to get them back. This directly affected my clients, and one of them intervened. I was able to pick them up a few days later. I didn't care that they searched all the hard drives and emails. There was nothing for either Patrick or myself to hide. I'm sure they were desperate to find something. Too bad for them.

My retired cop sister-in-law was on the grass with the garden hose trying to wash away Patrick's blood. She was talking to a few detectives outside. I was so glad all the news reporters finally gave up trying to get me to talk to them, and had since left. My parents and daughter wanted to stay with me overnight but I told them to go home. After they left I just sat there in the living room, staring at the mess of things that Patrick and I shared. Anxious thoughts raced through my mind. He's gone, he's really gone. He's never coming home. I cried so much I think I seriously dehydrated myself.

I cuddled my dogs, feeling so sorry that they went through this. Through his eyes I could see Emo crying inside. It didn't seem to sink in to Frito yet. He was a new dog that we had just rescued from being tied to a pole in the barrio, and hadn't yet bonded with Patrick like Emo had. Frito's energetic puppy playfulness helped to distract me from my immense despair. I don't know what I would have done without my loving dogs.

Patrick's younger brother told me that all of his life he knew that this day would come. He said it wasn't *if*—it was *when*. When Patrick and I got together I was determined to change all of that. But I didn't—I just delayed it for twenty years.

CHAPTER 18

The days that followed were a blur through my tears and exhaustion. I was crawling through an endless emotional marathon with no finish line. My voice was so hoarse from crying that I could barely speak. I couldn't eat. There was no kind of pain I knew of that I could compare it to. It felt terminal, crushing, something I would never heal from. It felt like part of me had actually died with Patrick. I felt like I was only partially present in everything I did after that. The day he died changed me forever. Even now, seven years later, things that happen to me that would make someone else totally ecstatic, feel numbed down to me. Like it's not real.

Family and friends hung out at my house all day and into the night for weeks. The house was in a complete upheaval after the *unwarranted* search warrant. My sisters and parents came over to organize and clean. I was overwhelmed with all of the things people were telling me that I had to do. I walked around in a daze, sleepwalking through a nightmare I couldn't wake up from.

A news reporter called on the phone. Without offering any words of condolence, she talked very fast, rudely commanding me to tell her my side of the story. She had no regard to how I was suffering from the horror that I witnessed. She just wanted the story. Her disgusting approach left me speechless. I hung up on her without saying anything. She called back. *CLICK.* I slammed the phone down. Fuck you!

The first thing I wanted to do was to get the guns out of the house. That meant somehow opening the safe. Though I had always hated it, the presence of it now was something I could no longer cohabitate with. Jim hired a specialist to get into the safe. The dude torched that thing for four hours before finally being able to open it. I was afraid that the intense sparks and heat might set off the ammunition I knew was inside. Patrick had over five thousand rounds. He was prepared for the civil unrest the conspiracy theories made him believe were sure to happen.

Thankfully the safe was torched open without exploding. There were layers of toxic dust all over everything in that room and in the surrounding areas of the house. I could tell it wasn't healthy to breathe. Once the safe was open, I stood aside and watched Patrick's sister evaluate the contents. She seemed pissed off that there wasn't money inside. I had no clue why, but whatever—I told her to just take all of the guns and everything out of there. I couldn't look at the guns. If there was money in there, I didn't care, I just wanted that thing and all that was in it out of my house.

The next day, my best friend and her bad-ass firefighter husband came to take the safe from the house and discard it at the landfill. He's a big, strong guy, but he couldn't balance it all by himself. My best friend was somehow endowed with superhuman strength that day. Both she and her husband *still* can't believe that they actually succeeded (by themselves) to lift that thing up into *and* out of the truck.

Everyone wanted to know what really happened. As I re-wound the story over and over again of everything that happened the week before, incuding the affair, I began to sort out my confusion. The more I told my family and close friends, the more anger I started feeling. Seeing all their reactions to what *really* happened—which *isn't* what the news reported—kindled the fire for justice.

I found out that a neighborhood kid had used his cellphone to record the incident, and then uploaded it to YouTube. I couldn't watch it until two years later. He was able to capture the shooter and some detectives, but he was unable to capture Patrick's position. However, the audio part ended up being useful.

The affair guy wanted to see me. I told him to go away, and to stay away. He disgusted me, and reminded me of how disgusting I was.

After a few days, I just wanted to be alone. With so many people being in the house and rehashing the events so many times I just didn't want to talk anymore. I was physically exhausted. I hadn't eaten anything since the strawberry Patrick gave me the night before he was murdered. I wasn't hungry. I dumped any remaining alcohol that I found in the house. The smell of it made me physically ill.

I thought that this all would have never happened if Patrick was sober. Combining alcohol with pills that can cause suicidal tendencies, it was the prescription for disaster. The alcohol demons permeated his behavior, cursed, conquered, and then killed him. It was their favorite weapon against him. They finally won.

CHAPTER 19

I had to go to the mortuary and sign papers. Patrick's parents and his sister were there and took charge. I had no experience at all with what I was facing, and was glad I had Patrick's family there to make decisions on behalf of Patrick. I was in a blind state of cluelessness.

I didn't want anyone close to me—my parents, my daughter, or anyone else there with me because I didn't want to see them cry. I didn't want my pain to impact anyone else's life. It was my journey, one that I wanted to endure alone, as punishment and shame to myself.

I sat there overwhelmed with a bunch of papers in front of me. Although gravity kept them flat on the table to everyone else, to me everything in the room looked semi-transparent, and the papers sort of floated up and down off the table. My memory flashed back, seeing Patrick standing there facing the man that killed him, literally bearing the cross of his life in defeat. All my human senses were dulled, and another, deeper sense held me captive. It briefly made me understand something was much higher and profoundly better than all of this. It was then that Patrick said to me, "It's okay, I have a different body now." I felt his closeness; knew in some strange way that he was there in the room with us. In an intangible way this experience offered a weird, inexplicable sort of comfort.

Patrick's funeral and wake were combined. His body laid in an open casket. It didn't look like him. The sight of his unanimated body confirmed what I already knew—only his body is dead, not him. Remembering the first thing he told me in the sheriff station, when he clearly said to me, "THIS IS SO COOL!" I knew that his soul was overwhelmed with joy. But everyone he left behind wasn't, and many of them wouldn't understand the telepathy I had begun to receive. I didn't think they would believe me, but I told them anyway, because through me Patrick wanted to comfort them.

It is hard to explain to some people Patrick's way of communicating to me because many of them don't understand yet something I had just learned—that when we die it's just the body that we occupy here, not *us*. Patrick tells me things at times when I least expect, when I'm concentrating on other things entirely. I know that is how he gets me to understand that it's really him and not my imagination.

A lot of people from his work came to the funeral. Some of his long-time friends were there as well, including his now-famous pro-skater friend (the same guy that Patrick stole skateboards from in the '80s). Patrick's (forgiving) skater friend told me that his brother was a kick-ass attorney, and that he thought this incident should be a full-on lawsuit. I had never before thought of anything like that. He gave me his brother's contact information. I put it into my pocket. I didn't think much of it then.

After a few weeks when my friends and family receded back into their own lives, I was alone (as I ended up insisting), and that time gave me clarity and resolve. I was unsettled. It just wasn't right what happened to Patrick. I couldn't let it go as is. I saw it with my own eyes and IT WAS WRONG! Everything that happened that day was wrong. After a few weeks and a lot of prayer, I called the Skater Brother Attorney's office.

I went to a meeting downtown to give my statement. The more days that passed, the more I felt an incessant tugging for justice. The attorneys empowered me with confidence. It was a relief to know that others believed me and knew how to prove what really happened. That day I entered into a civil lawsuit claiming wrongful death. It was a stressful undertaking that was henceforth a part of my life for the next five years.

CHAPTER 20

In the course of those years, several *what ifs* inspired a lot of pensive reflection. I was alone and had a lot of time to think. During this time I also had a lot of time to grow like never before—as an individual and not a caretaker.

I felt guilty about the relief I felt knowing that I no longer had to worry about Patrick's well-being. I would for sure have him back if I could turn back time. I would have defiantly stuck to him all those years he told me to go away.

Did Patrick have to die that day? The killer never gave him a chance to decide. He made that decision for him, without first asking what he could do to help him.

The deputy that killed Patrick wasn't wearing a bodycam. If he were wearing a bodycam, it would have proved his heartless ignorance. Would he have still fired his assault rifle? Why didn't he give Patrick any warning—like "if you don't drop your weapon, I am going to shoot you?" There was *never* any warning. There was no intervention. The deputy's unprofessionalism is still implausible to me, as are his lies. This man stated in his deposition, "I'd do everything the same." Those words keep stinging me. I think it's his delusional pride talking in a frantic cover-up. If he really would have done the same things again, he is truly evil. Is this person really a human being?

I know that cops see a lot of really gruesome things and learn to handle them by becoming desensitized. It makes me wonder if the murderer didn't care that I would see my husband gush out blood and die from his senseless actions. Are they so desensitized by all the death they encounter that their own perpetration of it doesn't matter? Patrick was in a sacrificial stance. It looked to me like a surrender, his last effort to get the help that had always eluded him. I don't think he was expecting to die that day. He never said goodbye to his beloved animals. I wonder if Patrick would have said to the man that killed him "Thank you" or "Fuck you, I wasn't ready yet, why didn't you help me?" Knowing his theatrics, I tend to think the latter.

Seeing the way Patrick's murder hurt others deepened my own pain. It was horrible to witness how our beloved dogs were affected, especially Emo. I didn't know how to make them understand. I couldn't console them in any tangible way because there was no just reason why Patrick was gone. I wanted to keep both of them beside me all day and night. There was so much sadness in their eyes. They kept looking out the window and watching the door, waiting for Patrick to come home. It made the reality so much more devastating. My poor dogs. I cried so much for them because I could see their mourning manifested in their behavior.

I tried to distract my thoughts and focus on other things. I began to sleep on Patrick's side of the bed so that reaching out for him would feel different. Unexpectedly, this helped a lot. In an effort to concentrate on something else besides my writhing emptiness, I decided to focus on academic subjects that I wasn't good at. I read Patrick's biochemistry and astrophysics textbooks out loud to my dogs in a trying-to-be British accent, in order to force my mind not to wander back into haunting memories. It forced me to read slowly to articulate my very bad accent, and this helped the information sink in. I was laughing at myself, but learning at the same time.

One of my neighbors has a Honda that looks exactly like Patrick's. One day when I was out on our street walking Emo, we saw my neighbor's Honda driving around the culdesac and park. Emo ran up to it and circled around it, thinking Patrick had finally come home. When my neighbor got out and Emo realized that it wasn't Patrick, I burst into tears and ran to pick him up. I felt so weak with sorrow, I just sank to the sidewalk holding him. Emo's body was quivering. I could feel his pain. He was crying with me.

Sometimes I thought I couldn't handle the enormity of the devastation constantly shredding my heart. Literally my heart hurt, or that part of my body. It seemed like with every breath I took I couldn't get enough air. My chest always felt heavy and I was constantly sick to my stomach. I had no energy and didn't feel like doing anything. I wanted to sleep all the time to let my dreams take me somewhere else, only to awake to the horrible reality knowing that Patrick would be gone forever.

Several times I thought I would get on my board past the surfbreak and paddle into the horizon until I tired out, and then let the current take me wherever. Before I drifted to what would probably be somewhere in Baja, I might die from thirst, exposure or even better yet a shark misjudgment. I love sharks. I would love the fantastic adrenaline rush before my death. But I am comfortable around them so I wouldn't necessarily panic, and they might just bump me. If they were super hungry then they'd grab me because the shadow of my surfboard would look like a sea lion to them from below. I fantasized this as my first choice of how I would like to die.

I thought of taking my scuba gear to the calm water somewhere in the depths of the Caribbean fishtank, dive down to about fifty feet, and hang out there in that beautiful world, peacefully letting my air run out.

But my suicide would be traumatic for others. They've been through the dramatic death of Patrick, so why should I selfishly make it worse for them.

CHAPTER 21

Days turned into weeks, weeks turned into months and months dragged on to years. That was the "discovery" phase, during which time my attorneys obtained all of the defense's evidence, and hired various professionals to help substantiate our case.

I expected that the sheriffs were going to masterfully cover their asses. They did an expert job of editing the audio of my detainment. They produced as evidence just a little over two hours of my almost seven hour detainment. They professionally replaced everything they would not want a courtroom to hear with the sound of me crying. When I listened to the tapes, I was certain that they had been edited. I could tell that parts of my crying bouts were repeat recordings, having been spliced in at sections replacing what I remembered I was saying at the time. I asked my attorney to get an expert to find evidence of that. In a quick surface analysis he couldn't find any tampering. I knew for certain it was edited though, and if we had gone to trial I would have insisted on paying for a more in-depth review.

My attorneys had professional trajectory analysis done by comparing the entry and exit gunshot wounds on Patrick's body to the way he was standing when it happened. The results proved that there is no way Patrick could have sustained those same injuries while in the position(s) that Deputy 1 had described. The bullet entry and exit could only be possible by him being in the position that I had described.

The evidence proved that by his injuries Patrick was not sitting on the grass. Deputy 1 was lucky that the fun he was having with his AR-15 did not kill my neighbor or her toddler son she was holding as one of his stray bullets sped past them and struck a mattress in their bedroom.

The defense just wanted this case to go away. The attorneys on both sides knew that going to trial meant much more money being spent, and much more publicity and stress. Publicity like this would surely embarrass and shame local law enforcement. They would not like their godlike status to be defamed.

There were several hearings to try to settle the case before trial. The defense pled that they were entitled to "qualified immunity" and each time the courts refused to grant it. The defense wanted the courts to drop the charges, because according to them, they "did nothing wrong." But none of the judges would grant them immunity. In his deposition, Deputy 1 used the term "Suicide by Cop," which is in my opinion, a contradictory term that applies to them exclusively. This means that a cop is allowed to kill someone if that person asks them to? Suicide by definiton means the taking of one's own life. Adding *by cop* after that is a contradiction and serves as their excuse to commit homicide and get away with it. Will a law enforcement officer push someone off the Coronado Bridge if that person asked them to? Are they empowered by a badge-boasting right to murder? It's their own code of law, one not to protect and serve others, but to protect and serve *themselves.* They think they're always right, that they're above the law that they themselves corrupt.

Because of sensationalized media, the story of one bad cop can criminalize an entire force. I know that the actions of a few do not necessarily define the hearts of the rest. I don't think that most of them would murder someone just because they can't wait to use their assault rifle, and later say that they would do it all over again. How do these kind of individuals get the so-called privilege to protect us?

The person in uniform is an image we have been culturally manipulated to submit to. It falsely endows some of them with a status of infallibility, empowering them with an ill-perceived level of god-like superiority. It makes me wonder if this particular individual—priorly serving as a United States Marine trained to kill—should subsequently be fit for a job as a law enforcement officer with a duty that is supposedly the opposite?

I wanted to stand up in front of a jury and tell the truth of what I saw with my own eyes. That man murdered my loving husband of twenty years and thought he could just nonchalantly walk away. He said he would do it all over again. He would? *Really?* I didn't want this injustice to silently go away for them by settling out of court. I wanted this deputy to be held accountable for his actions, and I wanted everyone to see how it was covered up. It would still be my word against his, even though I know that Deputy 2 saw it too. In his deposition he stated that he didn't see it, but I saw him see it. It doesn't matter though, my word could have still lost over theirs. It would have only taken that one juror that thinks cops are always right.

In each of the settlement hearings, my attorneys and I offered to take a very reduced amount of money in exchange for ensuring that local law enforcement would receive a more extensive regime of training in addressing those who suffer from mental illness. We were consistently rebuffed. The defense defiantly said that they already had that in place. We *did* know they had that training already, we were just asking that they could implement more *thorough* training. I wanted them to learn from what happened to Patrick so that there would be much less of a chance of others suffering through a similar situation in the future.

In going to trial, the defense would pull out everything they could to shatter my character and make me look like a total whore. Furthermore, they would try to make it look like my incentive for pushing through with all this was financial. How could even a penny bring Patrick back home to me? My incentive was justice, and to dispel the lies. I was willing to be trashed. I had nothing to hide. However, I have no experience to begin to imagine the emotional torment I would have to endure in trial to defend the truth against the leeches who would try to suck out my soul.

CHAPTER 22

The following ballistics report is a summary that includes the defense's version of events compared to mine. It also shows that this was not an easy case. It would have only taken one juror to not believe my version for the murderer to walk free. But because the killer hid under the shield of his badge, he walked free anyway.

The following list of police and laboratory reports, photographs, witness statements, deputy statements, autopsy protocol and photographs, site inspection, evidence examinations and depositions were used by the undersigned as source material for the opinions and conclusions expressed in this report. The undersigned received flash drives on 11-7-16, 7-27-17 and 8-7-17contained the following material for review:

- Aerial photographs 1, 2 and 3
- Photos of bullet strikes to houses
- Cell phone video
- BCME Photographs
- BCME Reports
- BCSD Audio interview of Deputy 1
- BCSD Audio interview of Deputy 2
- BCSD Interview of Tim Warner
- BCSD Multiple audio interviews of witnesses
- BCSD Audio walk through with Deputy 1
- BCSD Audio walk through with Deputy 2
- BCSD Scene diagrams
- BCSD Diagrams – Deputy 1 interview
- BCSD Diagrams – Deputy 2 interview
- BCSD Autopsy Photos
- BCSD Processing photos of Deputy 1
- BCSD Processing photos of Deputy 2
- BCSD Scene photos 1, 2 and 3
- BCSD Search photos 1, 2 and 3
- BCSD Detective 2- 1 and 2 Autopsy
- BCSD Detective 3- reports 1, 2 &3
- BCSD Detective 1's reports 1, 2 &3

- Scene walk through on 3-1-17
- Examine the 12 Ga. Mossberg model 500A shotgun, serial # 400986 and Mr. Sharp's shorts at the BCSD on 3-1-17
- Examine the 5.56mm/.223 Rem caliber Smith & Wesson model M&P-15 semi-auto rifle, serial number ST50919
- Telephone conversation with Ms. Sharp
- Multiple other police reports
- Deposition of Deputy 1
- Deposition of Deputy 2
- Deposition of Ms. Sharp
- Multiple other depositions
- Pleadings and Discoveries

QUALIFICATIONS FOR OPINION

The opinions and conclusions reached on the above-mentioned shooting are based on the following:

- My review of all the above listed material and evidence.
- My experience as a Michigan State Police Officer for over 25 years rising to the rank of D/Lt. in charge of the Firearms, Tool-Mark and Bombs and Explosive Unit of the MSP Northville Forensic Science Laboratory.
- My experience for over 20 years as a member of the Michigan State Police Forensic Science Laboratory in the Firearms Identification, Tool Mark, Bombs and Explosive Unit.
- My experience with the Michigan State Police as a Crime Scene Analysis participating in and supervising hundreds of crime scene investigations during my years with the department.
- My experience at photographing and collecting evidence at crime scenes while with the Michigan State Police.
- My experience at photographing, participating in and collecting evidence at autopsies for over 20 years.
- Training sessions on crime scene reconstruction both as a member of the Michigan State Police and as a civilian examiner.
- My experience in investigating shooting crime scenes for over 20 years as a member of the Michigan State Police and then continuing to utilize that experience as a self-employed examiner in assessing shooting crime scenes for the past 25+ years.
- My experience at having examined hundreds of shooting victims at crime scenes, autopsies, hospitals and funeral homes.
- My experience at taking and interpreting X-Ray's in bomb squad work and training as well as at using and interpreting X-Ray's at crime scenes, autopsies and hospitals for the past 45+ years.
- See a copy of my C.V. for more specific information.

INFORMATION

The following is a brief description of the above shooting event as understood by the undersigned:

The (Beach City) Sheriff's Department received a 911 hang up call coming from (My Address) and assigned Deputy 2 to respond to the call. Deputy 1 also heard the call and was responding as well. Deputy 2 arrived near the location and was flagged down by a civilian, Mr. Timothy Warner, who proceeded to advise Deputy 2 that his neighbor, a Mr. Sharp, had just threatened to kill him with a shotgun. Mr. Sharp lived at (My Address) , the location of the 911 hang up call.

214

Deputy 2   broadcast that there is a man with a shotgun inside (my address) and that a female is also inside. Deputy 2   has been on the scene for about 5 minutes when Deputy 1   arrives. Deputy 1   has an AR-15 and charges the weapon while walking past Deputy 2   toward the garage area of the complex. Deputy 2   does not exchange any information with Deputy 1   at this time other than to point to the direction in which he believed the Sharp   residence to be located. Moments later, Deputy 2   hears Deputy 1   engaging an individual with commands of "put the gun down" or words to that effect and at this time Deputy 2   disengages from Mr. Warner and hurries to the position of Deputy 1   who is located at the corner of the garages to cover Deputy 1   . While going to this location, Deputy 2   hears several shots, he never sees Mr. Sharp   or the position of Mr. Sharp   when he was shot, he only sees Mr. Sharp   lying face down on the grass with his feet toward Deputy   1   's location.

Deputy 1   states that once he arrived at the corner of the garage area he observed Mr. Sharp   (Deputy 1   does not know this is Mr. Sharp   at this time) sitting in the grassy area essentially facing the   (My Address)   with the barrel of a shotgun near or under his chin. In this position, Mr. Sharp   had his left side facing Deputy 1   . Once Deputy 1   begins to give commands to Mr. Sharp   sitting on the grass, Mr. Sharp   gets to his feet and is holding the shotgun in his left hand by the forearm (slide) of the weapon with the barrel pointed straight up in the air. There is a large clear liquor bottle on the ground and nothing in Mr. Sharp 's right hand. Mr. Sharp   is standing with both arms outstretched to either side and parallel to the ground. Mr. Sharp   is reportedly yelling "shoot me" or words to that effect and at this time, according to Deputy 1   , Mr. Sharp   begins to transition the shotgun from vertical to pointing towards Deputy 1   . The shotgun never quite points at Deputy 1

before he fires three (3) shots, Mr. Sharp   falls backward, onto his back with his feet toward Deputy 1   . Deputy 1   then momentarily takes a knee and then stands back up in his original position. Deputy 1   states that at this point Mr. Sharp   then sits up and again begins to point the shotgun in the direction of Deputy 1   the same way he did the first time at which time he (1) fires one more shot and Mr. Sharp   falls to the grass on his face/side.

Ms. Sharp   stated that Mr. Sharp   walked out into the grassy area in front of their home and was holding the shotgun in his right hand and a vodka bottle in his left hand with his arms outstretched as previously described. Ms. Sharp   stated that when Mr. Sharp   dropped the vodka bottle from his left hand is when he was shot and that Mr. Sharp   was facing their home when the first shots were fired, he staggered and spun around and fell to the ground face first, briefly lifted his head and mouthed words to her and then his head fell to the ground. Ms. Sharp   states that Mr. Sharp   never was sitting in the grassy area, he always had the shotgun in his right hand, the vodka bottle in his left hand, he never pointed the shotgun at anyone and once he fell to the ground he never sat up.

The only two witnesses to the actual shooting are Deputy 1   and Ms. Sharp   .

COMMENTS AND OBSERVATIONS

The undersigned received all of the photographs taken on this case in a format that it was not possible to extract individual photographs and insert them in the body of my report to discuss specific points, therefore I will refer to specific photographs throughout my report, clearly identify these photographs and then attach copies of those photographs to my final report.

There are two (2) distinct versions of how this shooting took place. Ms. Sharp never has Mr. Sharp sitting on the grass prior to the shooting while he is holding the shotgun in his right hand by the forehand and at the same time holding the vodka bottle in his left hand with both arms stretched out and parallel to the ground. It is the dropping of the vodka bottle in her version of the event that has the shots being fired with Mr. Sharp turning, staggering and then falling face down on the grass. Mr. Sharp lifts his head up slightly to mouth words to Ms. Sharp, however he never sits up.

Deputy 1 has Mr. Sharp setting in the grass pointing the shotgun at his own head/chin, then getting up with the shotgun in his left hand by the forehand and with his arms outstretched and parallel to the ground as described by Ms. Sharp. However, in his version, Mr. Sharp suddenly transitions the shotgun with the barrel coming towards Deputy 1 's direction and this predicates the initial three (3) shots from Deputy 1 . After the third shot Deputy 1 goes to one knee for just a second and he gets back up. It is at this time that Deputy 1 sees Mr. Sharp sit up, again begin to move the shotgun to point it at Deputy 1 and Deputy 1 fires one (1) more shot with Mr. Sharp falling to his side/face. Deputy 1 states that he fired all four (4) of his shots while standing. It should be noted that there is a cell phone video that shows a deputy where Block places himself at the scene, on his right knee, holding a long gun for several seconds pointed parallel to the ground in the direction of Mr. Sharp .

There were four (4) shots fired by Deputy 1 and there were only two (2) bullet strikes to Mr. Sharp . The fatal wound, listed as wound #2, enters the back of Mr. Sharp 's left triceps centered 8-1/8" below the shoulder and approximately 17" from the top of the head. The pathologist does not indicate angle; however, this bullet is traveling at a dramatically upward angle through the left arm, with the exit centered 6" from the left shoulder, which I see as approximately 2 1/8" above the bullet's entry point. This bullet then re-enters Mr. Sharp 's left chest, also centered 6" from the shoulder, and travels rightward, slightly upward and minimally forward. This describes a bullet traveling virtually straight and level into the chest.

Deputy 1 demonstrated several times during his video deposition as to how Mr. Sharp maneuvered the shotgun into a position where it was almost (and sometimes was) pointing at Deputy 1 when he fired his weapon. The problem is that none of the positions shown by Deputy 1 could possibly explain the bullets' travel through Mr. Sharp . The triceps area is never exposed to the muzzle of Deputy 1 's rifle in any of Mr. Sharp's reported maneuvers as demonstrated by Deputy 1. Any person holding the forehand of a shotgun with their left hand cannot receive the bullet strike Mr. Sharp received in this case, because the angle of the bullet both - in the upper arm and subsequently into the chest - would be dramatically different.

The evidence clearly shows that the bullet entry into Mr. Sharp's left triceps had to have taken place when he (Mr. Sharp) was holding his arms close to parallel to the ground in an outstretched manner as describe by both Deputy 1 and Ms. Sharp. Any person holding the forehand of a shotgun with their left hand and the pistol grip with their right hand to allow the barrel to be close to parallel to the ground while pointing/swinging the muzzle towards Deputy 1's position, could not have received the bullet strike Mr. Sharp received in his triceps, because the angle of the bullet - both in the upper arm and subsequently into the chest - would be dramatically different. The evidence clearly shows that the bullet entry into Mr. Sharp's left triceps had to happen when he was holding his arms parallel to the ground in an outstretched manner in this examiner's opinion. This position explains the dramatic upward angle through the upper arm while allowing the bullet to travel rightward, slightly upward and minimally forward into the chest.

The other bullet strike to Mr. Sharp, wound #1, was a superficial wound to his right side which the pathologist stated was nearly horizontal. However, the pathologist was unable to determine the direction of travel. This bullet strike is important for several reasons. First, even though the pathologist did not give an exact location for this wound from the top of the head, it is clearly evident that this strike is only 3-5" below the entry wound to the left chest of Mr. Sharp and parallel to the ground for a standing person. This indicates that this wound was received about the same time as the fatal wound. With a standing Deputy 1 firing at a standing Mr. Sharp, the graze wound could be the 1st, 2nd or 3rd shot depending on how Mr. Sharp reacted to the fatal wound, which had to have been delivered while Mr. Sharp was standing upright with his arms outstretched. If wound #1 was the first injury to Mr. Sharp, then he would have been totally facing towards Deputy 1 or had his back entirely toward Deputy 1 when this injury occurred. Another problem that I see with the graze injury to Mr. Sharp's right side is that in all of the demonstrations shown by Deputy 1 the area of the graze wound (Mr. Sharp's right side) has most of the shotgun and his right arm covering this area. It is unlikely that this bullet strike could have occurred without hitting the shotgun or Mr. Sharp's right arm.

The two residences (located at 1957 and 1955 Address) were each struck by one of the bullets fired by Deputy 1. With the bullet recovered from Mr. Sharp's body at the autopsy, that accounts for three (3) of the fired bullets and leaves one (1) fired bullet unaccounted for in this shooting. One of the two bullets striking the residences may also have been responsible for the graze injury to Mr. Sharp. However, the only way to know would have been to have examined these fired bullets for DNA material, which did not happen. What is more, the bullet striking 1955 Address (listed as strike A) was

Deputy 1's version

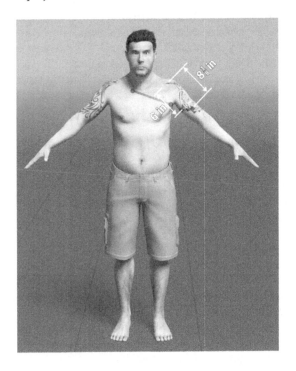

not even recovered, apparently for cosmetic reasons. The bullet striking 1957 Address (listed as strike B), which travelled into one of the residence's bedrooms, was on a direct line from the corner of the garage where Deputy 1 was firing when I checked the trajectory using a laser. Even though this bullet struck in an upstairs bedroom, the topography of the area allowed for a direct bullet strike from the corner of the garage. See attached photograph labeled # 1.

The bullet strike (listed as strike A) to a post area of 1955 Address was approximately 3-4 feet below where bullet strike (B) impacted 1957 Address . However, these two bullet strikes were only approximately 6-10" side to side from each other. In examining bullet strike (A) in the post, the undersigned was only able to contact this hole with the laser from the corner of the garage where deputy 1 was firing if I were standing and pointing the laser as one would fire a rifle from their shoulder.

The 2nd report of Detective 1 , which containing autopsy photographs, reportedly shows how the pathologist used a plastic trajectory rod to confirmed the account of the shooting as given by Deputy 1 . However, this demonstration using the trajectory rod is totally inaccurate and misleading. The photograph detective 1 uses to make this point is one where Mr. Sharp 's left arm is directly against his left chest wall. When closely examining this photograph, the trajectory rod is on a dramatic upward path, not at all what was reported in the autopsy protocol. More importantly, it is very obvious that the autopsy has been completed and that the chest cavity is still open with the two sections of chest tissue some 3-5 inches apart (specifically the center of Mr. Sharp 's chest towards his left shoulder), thus making any determination of bullet travel through the body highly speculative and questionable.

The use of a trajectory rod to determine the bullets flight path through the body should have been done prior to the chest being opened for an accurate determination. However, had the pathologist done that, the only way that the trajectory rod could have been inserted through the left triceps and into the chest, would have been with the left arm of Mr. Sharp some distance from the chest entry hole and parallel to his feet. Confirmation of this can be seen when viewing several of the autopsy photographs where the left arm is away from the left chest with the trajectory rod still in both the arm and chest. The obvious dramatic pulling of the skin tissue around the exit wound in the upper arm clearly shows that this was not the bullet's flight path. There were no photographs depicting the skin around the trajectory rod at the re-entry hole in the left chest where it is likely that the skin would also have been stretched. Please refer to autopsy photographs #'s 74/112, 75/112, 79/112, 106/112 and 107/112. On the last two photographs, the trajectory rod is bent due the force required to show the suggested wound path. The attached photographs labeled #'s 2, 3, 4, 5 and 6 are the above listed photographs.

219

Superficial wound that spun him around

Fatal wound

OPINIONS AND CONCLUSIONS

The fatal bullet wound to Mr. Sharp had to have occurred while Mr. Sharp was sideways to Deputy 1 (exposing Mr. Sharp 's left side) and had at least his left arm away from his body and roughly parallel to the ground. Scene photographs, such as scene # 3 photo 166/187 depicting the inside of Mr. Sharp 's left upper arm and his left chest wall show blood spatter on both surfaces. If Mr. Sharp 's arm was against the chest wall as depicted by the pathologist, there would not have been a spatter pattern on both areas as shown in multiple photographs. Furthermore, if the two skin areas would have slapped together as suggested by the pathologist, this area of blood spatter would have been smeared. Rather this pattern was caused by the passage of a high-speed projectile causing a temporary cavity in the upper arm and left chest wall. See attached photograph labeled # 7.

The fatal wound, the graze wound and the bullet strike to 1957 Address into the upstairs bedroom all are consistent with the shooter firing his rifle parallel to the ground from a standing or kneeling position. However, the bullet strike to 1955 Address could only have been fired from a standing position, with the rifle pointed at a downward angle so that the bullet just misses the ground near where Mr. Sharp was located and strikes the post at 1955 Address . Neither of the bullet strikes to the houses appear to have been caused by bullets that were not stable in flight prior to impact with the structures. The fact that the bullet strike to the bedroom of 1957 Address travels on a very straight path through the wall, the mattress, strikes the door, the floor and finally the closet door, reinforce in this examiners opinion that the bullet had little to no damage prior to striking the outside wall.

The evidence clearly supports the version of the shooting event as told by Ms. Sharp and totally refutes the version of the shooting as told by Deputy 1 .

I reserve the right to change or modify any of the expresses opinions and conclusions if additional evidence is made available.

Respectfully submitted,

(Ballistics Expert)

221

CHAPTER 23

In the month that we were to have our last settlement hearing before going to trial, Covid-19 shut everything down, including my largest client. The courts closed. Instead of going to the courthouse, I went to my Attorney's office for an eight hour conference call with a judge, the defense attorney, and the County Board of Supervisors. Trial was the next step, because all of the defense's appeals for "Qualified Immunity" had been exhausted.

The conference call took forever. I think they wanted tire me out. I wasn't tired. I wanted to run the marathon to justice no matter how long it took. But there is no justice. No amount of money would bring Patrick back. But I knew he would want me to fight to make them culpable, so that the cops can learn from the mistakes they made that day and hopefully not let this ever happen again to anyone else.

I knew that if we didn't have a settlement that day I would have to wait until the courts opened again to resume the progress toward trial. But the reality was, I lost my work for who knows how long. I lived alone. How was I going to be able to pay for all of my insurance and my mortgage? The Covid thing was so scary and uncertain. I decided to settle and get it over with. In doing so, and in perfect cue with the Covid lockdown, the settlement legally released me to share the entirety of Patrick's story. My jobless days gave me all the time I needed to start writing.

This book was very hard to write, forcing me to relive horrific memories. Even so, I was compelled to do it for Patrick. As time passed, deeper revelations made me see that what had happened to him could be used for a higher purpose and for the good of others. I did not want Patrick's unjust death to go without telling the true story of the way he suffered through life. He would have wanted to help people with mental health issues to effectively dodge the bullets fired at them from the standpoint of ignorance. I hope that this book helps shatter that ignorance.

Patrick blessed so many other people's lives with his kindness. He gave over and over again without a second thought. Going through life with him left a lasting impression me, something that has permanently inspired and transformed me.

Made in the USA
Las Vegas, NV
04 February 2022

43134600R00125